Crochet Amigurumi Baby Animals

Patterns to Create Adorable Critters Animal Friends

COMPLETE GUIDE TO CROCHET TOYS TECHNIQUES MADE EASY

Volume 6
Patterns by Sevda Bebek

Edit by

Magic Knit

Publish by

Daring LTD

ISBN: 9798372107922

Content

Lady Bunny page 3
Fishing Cat page 9
Handsome Boy dog page 15 Pinky
Francy Girl Dog page 21
Easter Bunny page 27
Cute Dino Eating Spaghetti page 33
Cute Elephant page 39
Mushroom Picking Bear page 46
Teddy Bear Pen Holder page 52
Winter Cat page 58
Cute Mokey page 65
Ice Snowman page 70

Dear Customer
I am on emerging editor and, with the sales made by the book,
I can continue my studies to publish
other books on the subject.
I would appreciate on honest review from you. Also, please if
you notice any mistakes or missing
information, feel free to contact me at this
e-mail address: wwwanacraft@gmail.com
Thank you for your support

write to us to get extra free content for you

https://forms.gle/BoTwQKSR3nwhHc2X9

Lady Bunny

Abbreviation/US terminology :

blo	-	back loop
ch	-	chain
cr	-	crochet
dc	-	double crochet
dc3tog	-	double crochet three together
dec	-	decrease
flo	-	front loop
hdc	-	half double crochet
FO	-	Fasten Off
inc	-	increase
rnd(s)	-	round(s)
sc	-	single crochet
sc3tog	-	single crochet three together
slst	-	slip stitch
st	-	stitch
tr	-	treble stitch
(...)	-	number in parentheses indicates the number of stitches at the end of the round
[...]	-	repeat instructions x times or to the end of the round
(...)	-	work the stitches all into the same stitch

You are welcome to sell items made from this pattern. I would be happy if you link back to my shop and give credit to me as the designer.

Materials:

- Yarn
- 2.5 mm hook size or a size that fits your yarn
- Scissors, stuffing, tapestry needle, stitch marker and pins

Main Color: Soft Pink **A:** Soft Green **B:** Dark Pink

C: Smoked color **D:** Orange color (green color between the legs)

FINISHED SIZE
Around 20 cm in circumference, about 10 cm in length.

LEGS AND TORSO

Round-1- 8 sc in a magic ring

Round 2- 8 sc inc(16 sc)

Round 3- 5 sc into sc(5 sc inc)6 sc into sc(21 sc)

Round 4-6- (3 ring)sc into sc(21 sc)

Round 7- 6 sc into sc(5 sc dec)6 sc into sc(16 sc)

Round 8- 6 sc into sc(2 sc dec)6 sc into sc(14 sc)

Round 9-11- (3 ring)sc into sc(14 sc) Ana color

Round 12- Only in flo sc into sc(14 sc)

Round 13-21- (9 ring)sc into sc(14 sc)

Round 22- Put the legs together, make 2 ch together. sc into sc(30 sc)

Tightly stuff the legs. Keep filling as you go.

Round 23- 14 sc into sc(2 ch into 4 sc)14 sc into sc(32 sc)

Round 24-26- (3 ring)sc into sc(32 sc)

A COLOR

Round 27- (4 times)6 sc into sc next inc(36 sc)

Round 28-35- (8 ring)sc into sc (36 sc)

Round 36- (6 times)5 sc into sc next dec(30 sc)

Round 37- Sc into sc (30 sc)

Round 38- (6 times)5 sc into sc next dec(24 sc)

Round 39- Sc into sc(24 sc)

Round 40- Only in flo sc into sc(24 sc)

Round 41- Only in blo sc into 3 ch fo

EARS

EARS (Make 2)

Main color

Round 1- 6 sc in a magic ring

Round 2- (3 times)1 sc into sc next inc(9 sc)

Round 3- (3 times)2 sc into sc next inc(12 sc)

Round 4- (2 times)5 sc into sc next inc(14 sc)

Round 5- (2 times)6 sc into sc next inc(16 sc)

Round 6- (2 times)7 sc into sc next inc(18 sc)

Round 7- (2 times)8 sc into sc next inc(20 sc)

Round 8-17- (10 ring)sc into sc(20 sc)

Round 18- (4 times)4 sc into sc next dec(16 sc)

Round 19- Sc into sc(16 sc)fo.

Leave a long thread end for sewing.

ARMS

ARMS (Make 2)

Main Color

Round 1- 5 ch.ch into sc(10 sc)

Round 2-5- (4 ring)sc into sc(10 sc)

Round 6- 5 sc into sc 2 ch. 2 ch into sc 5 sc into sc

Round 7- 2 ch out next 10 sc into sc

Round 8- (4 times)2 sc into sc next dec (6 sc)

Round 9- (4times)2 sc into sc next inc(10 sc)

Round 10- (4 times)3 sc into sc next inc(14 sc)

A COLOR

Round 11- Only in flo sc into sc(14 sc)

Round 12-22- (11 ring)sc into sc(14 sc)fo.

Straighten. Dip the crochet in both layers. (7 sc) fo.

Leave a long thread end for sewing.

HEAD

Main Color

Round 1- 6 sc in a magic ring

Round 2- 6 sc inc(12 sc)

Round 3- 1 sc into sc next inc(18 sc)

Round 4- 2 sc into sc next inc(24 sc)

Round 5- 3 sc into sc next inc(30 sc)

Round 6- 4 sc into sc next inc(36 sc)

Round 7- 5 sc into sc next inc(42 sc)

Round 8- 6 sc into sc next inc(48 sc)

Round 9-14- (6 ring)sc into sc(48 sc)

Round 15- 11 sc into sc(3 sc inc)20 sc into sc(3 sc inc)11 sc into sc(54 sc)

Round 16- Sc into sc(54 sc)

Round 17- 13 sc into sc(3 sc inc)22 sc into sc(3 sc inc)13 sc into sc(60 sc)

Round 18-21- (4 ring)sc into sc(60 sc)

Round 22- 8 sc into sc next dec(54 sc)

Round 23- 7 sc into sc next dec(48 sc)

Round 24- 6 sc into sc next dec(42 sc)

Round 25- 5 sc into sc next dec (36 sc)

Round 26- 4 sc into sc next dec(30 sc)

Fill the head tightly.

Round 27- 3 sc into sc next dec(24 sc)

Round 28- 2 sc into sc next dec(18 sc)

Round 29- Sc into sc (18 sc)fo.

Leave a long thread end for sewing.

RABBIT'S DRESS

B COLOR

Round 1- 40 ch.

Round 2- 40 ch into sc(40 sc)

Round 3-4- (2 ring)sc into sc (40 sc)

Round 5- Sc into 2 ch(80 cr)

Round 6-8- (3 ring)cr into cr (80 cr)

Round 9-10- (2 ring)cr into sc(80 sc)

Round 11- Only in blo sc into sc(80 sc)fo.

CLOTHES HANGERS (Make 2)

30 ch.ch into sc (30 sc) fo.

Leave a long thread end for sewing.

BASKET & CARROTS

Round 1- 8 sc in a magic ring

Round 2- 8 sc inc(16 sc)

Round 3- 1 sc into sc next inc(24 sc)

Round 4- 2 sc into sc next inc(32 sc)

Round 5- Only in flo sc into sc(32 sc)

Round 6-11 (6 ring)sc into sc(32 sc)

Round 12- Basket hanger - 20 ch.

Round 13- 20 ch into 20 sc fo.

CARROT

D COLOR

Round 1- 8 sc in a magic ring

Round 2-8- (7 ring)sc into sc(8 sc)

Round 9- 1 sc dec(7 sc)

Round 10- 1 sc dec(6 sc)

Round 11- 1 sc dec(5 sc)

Round 12- 1 sc dec (4 sc)

Round 13- 1 sc dec(3 sc)fo.

MAKING OF THE PARTS

FLOWERS

DRESS FLOWER (MAKE 3)

8 sc in a magic ring fo. Leave a long thread end for sewing.

CORONET (MAKE 3)

10 ch. 1 ch into 3 cr 1 ch into 1 sc(15 cr 5 sc) Fo. Leave a long thread end for sewing.

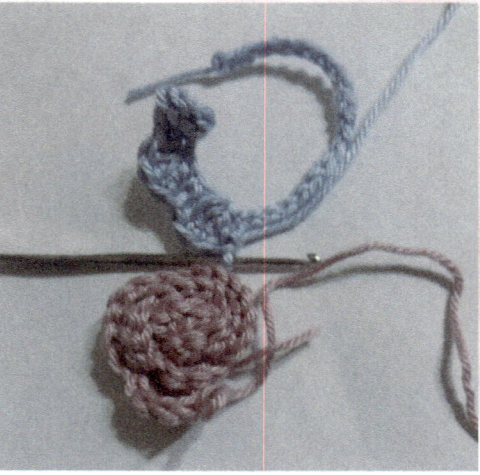

Fishing Cat

Abbreviation/US terminology :

blo	-	back loop
ch	-	chain
cr	-	crochet
dc	-	double crochet
dc3tog	-	double crochet three together
dec	-	decrease
flo	-	front loop
hdc	-	half double crochet
FO	-	Fasten Off
inc	-	increase
rnd(s)	-	round(s)
sc	-	single crochet
sc3tog	-	single crochet three together
slst	-	slip stitch
st	-	stitch
tr	-	treble stitch
(...)	-	number in parentheses indicates the number of stitches at the end of the round
[...]	-	repeat instructions x times or to the end of the round
(...)	-	work the stitches all into the same stitch

You are welcome to sell items made from this pattern. I would be happy if you link back to my shop and give credit to me as the designer.

Materials:

- Yarn
- 2.5 mm hook size or a size that fits your yarn
- Scissors, stuffing, tapestry needle, stitch marker and pins

Main Color: White **A:** Mustard **B:** Light Green **C:** Red
D: Lily colour **E:** Orange

FINISHED SIZE
Around 20 cm in circumference, about 10 cm in length.

Fishing Cat

HEAD

Round 1- 6 sc in a magic ring

Round 2- 6 Main color-3 sc inc (6 sc)A color-3 sc inc(6)12 sc.

Round 3- Main color-(3 times)sc into sc next inc(9)A color-(3 times)sc into sc next inc(9)18 sc.

Round 4- (3 times)2 sc into sc next inc(12)A color-(3 times)2 sc into sc next inc(12)24 sc.

Round 5- Main color-(3 times)3 sc into sc next inc(15)A color(3 times)3 sc into sc next inc(15)30 sc.

Round 6- Main color-(3 times)4 sc into sc next inc(18)A color (3 times)4 sc into sc next inc(18)36 sc.

Round 7- Main color-(3 times)5 sc into sc next inc(21)A color(3 times)5 sc into sc next inc(21)42 sc.

Round 8- Main color-(3 times)6 sc into sc next inc(24)A color(3 times)6 sc into sc next inc(24)48 sc.

Round 9- Main color-24 sc into sc A color-24 sc into sc(48 sc)

Round 10- 21 sc into sc A color 27 sc into sc (48 sc)

Round 11- Main color-18 sc into sc A color 30 sc into sc(48 sc)

Round 12- Main color-15 sc into sc A color 33 sc into sc(48 sc)

Round 13- A color-48 sc into sc

Attach the safe eyes between the rings 15-16 with 9 sc between them.

Round 14-16- (3 ring)sc into sc (48 sc)

Round 17- 12 sc into sc(9 sc inc)6 sc into sc(9 sc inc)12 sc into sc(66 sc)

Round 18-21- (4 ring)sc into sc(66 sc)

Round 22- (6 times)9 sc into sc next dec(60 sc)

Round 23- (6 times)8 sc into sc next dec(54 sc)

Round 24- (6 times)7 sc into sc next dec(48 sc)

Round 25- (6 times)6 sc into sc next dec(42 sc)

Round 26- (6 times)5 sc into sc next dec(36 sc)

Round 27- (6 times)4 sc into sc next dec(30 sc)

Stuff the head tightly. Keep filling as you go.

Round 28- (6 times)3 sc into sc next dec(24 sc)

Round 29- sc into sc(24 sc) FO.

Leave a long thread end to sew.

EARS

(Make 2)

Round 1- A color-6 sc in a magic ring

Round 2- 6 sc inc(12 sc)

Round 3- sc into sc(12 sc)

Round 4- (6 times)1 sc into sc next inc(18 sc)

Round 5- sc into sc(18 sc)

Round 6-8- (3 ring)sc into sc(18 sc)fo.

Leave a long thread end for sewing.

ARMS

(Make 2)

Main Color

Round 1- 6 sc in a magic ring

Round 2- 6 sc inc(12 sc)

Round 3-7- (5 ring)sc into sc(12 sc)

B color-

Round 8- only in flo sc into sc (12 sc)

Round 9- (2 times)5 sc into sc next inc(14 sc)

Round 10-22- (13 ring)sc into sc(14 sc)fo.

Leave a long thread end for sewing.

Arm Detail

Round-6- only in blo sc into sc fo.

LEGS

(Make 2)

A Color

Round 1- 6 sc in a magic ring

Round 2- 6 sc inc(12 sc)

Round 3- sc into sc (12 sc)

Round 4- Only in flo sc into sc(12 sc)

Round 5-9- (5 ring)sc into sc (12 sc)

Main Color

Round 10- (2 times)5 sc into sc next inc(14 sc)

Round 11-19- (9 ring)sc into sc(14 sc)

Joining of Legs - Body

Round 20- 14 sc into sc 5 ch 14 sc into sc

Round 21- 5 ch into 5 sc 14 sc into sc. to the unworked rings of ch 5 sc 14 sc(38 sc)

Round 22-31- (10 ring)sc into sc(38 sc)

B Color

Round 32-38- (7 ring)sc into sc(38 sc)

Round 39- (6 times)4 sc into sc next dec(32 sc)

Round 40- (6 times)3 sc into sc next dec((26 sc)

Round 41- (6 times)2 sc into sc next dec(20 sc)fo.

CAT'S OUTFIT

C COLOR - MAKE 2

Round 1- 20 ch.

Round 2- 20 ch into 20 sc

Round 3-6- (4 ring)sc into sc(20 sc)

Round 7- Fold it. Dip the needle into both layers. (sc into sc(20 sc)

Round 8-11- (4 ring)sc into sc(20 sc)

Round 12- Bring the legs together. sc into sc (40 sc)

Round 13-17- (5 ring)sc into sc(40 sc)

Round 18- 34 sc into sc 6 ch. Skip 6 sc

Round 19-26- (8 ring)sc into sc(40 sc)fo.

Round 27- Mark the middle of the outfit. 8 sc into sc

Round 28- Turn 8 sc into sc.18 ch. Turn 18 ch into 18 sc fo.

Leave a long thread end to sew.

BASKET

Round 1- 6 sc in a magic ring

Round 2- 6 sc inc(12 sc)

Round 3- 1 sc into sc next inc(18 sc)

Round 4- 2 sc into sc next inc(24 sc)

Round 5- 3 sc into sc next inc(30 sc)

Round 6- Only in flo sc into sc(30 sc)

Round 7-10- (4 ring)sc into sc(30 sc)

Round 11- 1 ch 1 sc atla 1 sc into 2 hdc (15 ch)(15 hdc)

Round 12- 40 ch. Straighten the basket.

Insert the needle fully across. 40 ch into 40 sc fo.

FISH

MAIN COLOR - MAKE 4

Round 1- 6 sc in a magic ring

Round 2- (2 times)1 sc inc 2 sc into sc(8 sc)

Round 3- sc into sc(8 sc)

Round 4- C-color 3 sc into sc next inc 4 sc into sc(9 sc)

Round 5- 6 (2 ring)sc into sc (9 sc)

Round 7- 3 sc into sc next dec 4 sc into sc(8 sc)

Do not stuff the fish too tightly.

Round 8- (2 times)2 sc into sc next dec(6 sc)

Round 9- Main color 6 sc inc (12 sc) fo.

Handsome Dog

Abbreviation/US terminology :

blo	-	back loop
ch	-	chain
cr	-	crochet
dc	-	double crochet
dc3tog	-	double crochet three together
dec	-	decrease
flo	-	front loop
hdc	-	half double crochet
FO	-	Fasten Off
inc	-	increase
rnd(s)	-	round(s)
sc	-	single crochet
sc3tog	-	single crochet three together
slst	-	slip stitch
st	-	stitch
tr	-	treble stitch
(...)	-	number in parentheses indicates the number of stitches at the end of the round
[...]	-	repeat instructions x times or to the end of the round
(...)	-	work the stitches all into the same stitch

You are welcome to sell items made from this pattern. I would be happy if you link back to my shop and give credit to me as the designer.

Materials:

- Yarn
- 2.5 mm hook size or a size that fits your yarn
- Scissors, stuffing, tapestry needle, stitch marker and pins

Main Color: Mustard **A:** White **B:** Light Green **C:** Dark Green
D: Brown

FINISHED SIZE
Around 20 cm in circumference, about 10 cm in length.

Handsome Dog

HEAD

Main Color

Rnd 1- 6 sc in a magic ring

Rnd 2- 6 sc inc(12 sc)

Rnd 3- (6 times)1 sc into sc next inc(18 sc)

Rnd 4- (6 times)2 sc into sc next inc(24 sc)

Rnd 5- (6 times)3 sc into sc next inc(30 sc)

Rnd 6- (6 times)4 sc into sc next inc(36 sc)

Rnd 7- (6 times)5 scinto sc next inc(42 sc)

Rnd 8- (6 times)6 sc into sc next inc(48 sc)

Rnd 9-17- (9 ring)sc into sc(48 sc) Install the safety eyes between rnd 15-16. There will be 9 sc in between.

Rnd 18- 12 sc into sc (9 sc inc)6 sc into sc (9 sc inc)12 sc into sc(66 sc)

A Color

Rnd 19-26- (8 ring)sc into sc(66 sc)

Stuff the head tightly. Keep filling as you go.

Rnd 27- (6 times)9 sc into sc next dec(60 sc)

Rnd 28- (6 times)8 sc into sc next dec(54 sc)

Rnd 29- (6 times)7 sc into sc next dec(48 sc)

Rnd 30- (6 times)6 sc into sc next dec(42 sc)

Rnd 31- (6 times)5 sc into sc next dec(36 sc)

Rnd 32- (6 times)4 sc into sc next dec(30 sc)

Rnd 33- (6 times)3 sc into sc next dec(24 sc)

Rnd 34- Sc into sc (24 sc)fo. Leave a long thread for sewing.

LEGS

A Color - Make 2

Rnd 1- 6 sc in a magic ring

Rnd 2- 6 sc inc(12 sc)

Rnd 3- (6 times)1 sc into sc next inc(18 sc)

Rnd 4- only in flo sc into sc(18 sc)

Rnd 5-8- (4 ring)sc into sc (18 sc)

Main Color

Rnd 9-20 (12 ring)sc into sc(18 sc)

Rnd 21- Bring the legs together. make 4 ch in between.

Rnd 22- 18 sc into sc 4 ch into sc 18 sc into sc ch next ring 4 sc(44 sc)

Rnd 23-29- (7 ring)sc into sc(44 sc)

Rnd 30- (6 times)6 sc into sc next dec(38 sc)

B Color

Rnd 31-37- (7 ring)sc into sc(38 sc)

Rnd 38- (6 times)4 sc into sc next dec(32 sc)

Rnd 39- 2 times)14 sc into sc next dec(30 sc)

Rnd 40-43- (4 ring)sc into sc(30 sc)fo.

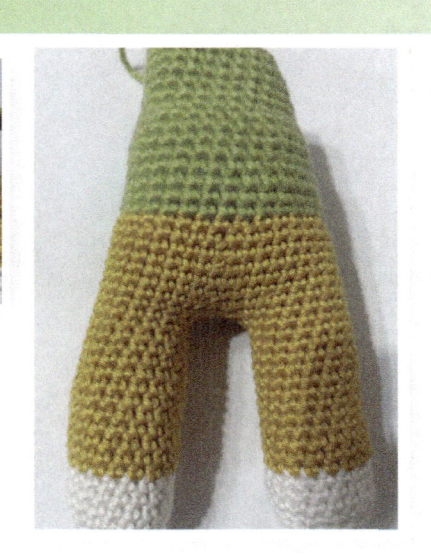

ARMS

Main Color - Make 2

Rnd 1- 6 sc in a magic ring

Rnd 2- 6 sc inc(12 sc)

Rnd 3-6- (4 ring)sc into sc (12 sc)

Rnd 7- Only in flo sc into sc(12 sc)

B Color

Rnd 8-22- (15 ring)sc into sc(12 sc)

Rnd 23- Flatten the needle in both layers.

6 sc fo. Do not fill the sleeves.

Arms Detail - Only in blo sc into 3 ch fo.

OVERALLS

C Color - Make 2

Rnd 1- 20 ch

Rnd 2- 20 ch into sc(20 sc)

Rnd 3-11- (9 ring)sc into sc(20 sc)fo.

Rnd 12- Bacakları birleştirin. sc into sc(40 sc)

Rnd 13-22- (10 ring)sc into sc (40 sc)

Rnd 23- 24 sc into sc turn

Rnd 24- 8 sc into sc turn

Rnd 25- 8 sc into sc fo.

Hangers - Make 2.

18 ch 18 ch into 18 sc fo.

Leave a long thread for sewing.

POCKETS

C Color - Make 2

Rnd 1- 5 ch .5 ch into 5 sc turn

Rnd 2- sc into sc(5 sc)turn

Rnd 3- sc into sc (5 sc)fo.

Leave a long thread for sewing

NOSE and NOSE TIP

NOSE TIP - D Color

Rnd 1- 2 ch into 2 sc turn

Rnd 2- 1 sc inc 2 sc into sc (3 sc)turn

Rnd 3- 1 sc inc 3 sc into sc(4 sc)turn

Rnd 4- 1 sc inc 4 sc into sc(5 sc)turn

Rnd 5- 1 sc inc 5 sc into sc(6 sc)fo.

Leave a long thread for sewing.

NOSE - A color

Rnd 1- 5 ch ch into sc(10 sc)

Rnd 2- 1 sc inc 4 sc into sc 1 sc inc(12 sc)

Rnd 3- 1 sc inc 5 sc into sc 1 sc inc (14 sc)

Rnd 4- 1 sc inc 6 sc into sc 1 sc inc(16 sc)

Rnd 5- 1 sc inc 7 sc into sc 1 sc inc(18 sc)fo.

Fill the nose, leave a long thread for sewing.

Sew the nose between the 2 eyes between Rnd 16-20. fo.

EARS

D COLOR - MAKE 2

Rnd 1- 6 sc in a magic ring

Rnd 2- 6 sc inc(12 sc)

Rnd 3- (6 times)1 sc into sc next inc(18 sc)

Rnd 4- (6 times)2 sc into sc next inc(24 sc)

Rnd 5- (6 times)3 sc into sc next inc(30 sc)

Rnd 6-10- (5 ring)sc into sc(30 sc)

Rnd 11- (6 times)3 sc into sc next dec(24 sc)

Rnd 12-15- (4 ring)sc into sc (24 sc)

Rnd 16- (6 times)2 sc into sc next dec(18 sc)

Rnd 17-21- (5 ring)sc into sc(18 sc)

Rnd 22- Flatten the needle in both layers. 9 sc fo.

Leave a long thread for sewing.

QUEUE

D Color

Rnd 1- 6 sc in a magic ring

Rnd 2- 6 sc inc(12 sc)

Rnd 3- (3 times)3 sc into sc next inc(15 sc)

Rnd 4-6- (3 ring)sc into sc(15 sc)

Rnd 7- (3 times)3 sc into sc next dec(12 sc)

Rnd 8-12 (5 ring)sc into sc(12 sc)

Rnd 13- (4 times)1 sc into sc next dec(8 sc)

Rnd 14-15- (2 ring)sc into sc(8 sc)

Rnd 16- Flatten the needle in both layers. 4 sc fo. Leave a long thread for sewing.

DETAILS

Fancy Dog

Abbreviation/US terminology :

blo	-	back loop
ch	-	chain
cr	-	crochet
dc	-	double crochet
dc3tog	-	double crochet three together
dec	-	decrease
flo	-	front loop
hdc	-	half double crochet
FO	-	Fasten Off
inc	-	increase
rnd(s)	-	round(s)
sc	-	single crochet
sc3tog	-	single crochet three together
slst	-	slip stitch
st	-	stitch
tr	-	treble stitch
(...)	-	number in parentheses indicates the number of stitches at the end of the round
[...]	-	repeat instructions x times or to the end of the round
(...)	-	work the stitches all into the same stitch

You are welcome to sell items made from this pattern. I would be happy if you link back to my shop and give credit to me as the designer.

Materials:

- Yarn
- 2.5 mm hook size or a size that fits your yarn
- Scissors, stuffing, tapestry needle, stitch marker and pins

Main Color: Mustard **A:** White **B:** Pink **C:** Red
D: Light Pink **E:** Lily **F:** Brown

FINISHED SIZE
Around 20 cm in circumference, about 10 cm in length.

Fancy Dog

HEAD

Main Color

Rnd 1- 6 sc in a magic ring

Rnd 2- 6 sc inc(12 sc)

Rnd 3- (6 times)1 sc into sc next inc(18 sc)

Rnd 4- (6 times)2 sc into sc next inc(24 sc)

Rnd 5- (6 times)3 sc into sc next inc(30 sc)

Rnd 6- (6 times)4 sc into sc next inc(36 sc)

Rnd 7- (6 times)5 scinto sc next inc(42 sc)

Rnd 8- (6 times)6 sc into sc next inc(48 sc)

Rnd 9-17- (9 ring)sc into sc(48 sc) Install the safety eyes between rnd 15-16. There will be 9 sc in between.

Rnd 18- 12 sc into sc (9 sc inc)6 sc into sc (9 sc inc)12 sc into sc(66 sc)

A Color

Rnd 19-26- (8 ring)sc into sc(66 sc)

Stuff the head tightly. Keep filling as you go.

Rnd 27- (6 times)9 sc into sc next dec(60 sc)

Rnd 28- (6 times)8 sc into sc next dec(54 sc)

Rnd 29- (6 times)7 sc into sc next dec(48 sc)

Rnd 30- (6 times)6 sc into sc next dec(42 sc)

Rnd 31- (6 times)5 sc into sc next dec(36 sc)

Rnd 32- (6 times)4 sc into sc next dec(30 sc)

Rnd 33- (6 times)3 sc into sc next dec(24 sc)

Rnd 34- Sc into sc (24 sc)fo. Leave a long thread for sewing.

ARMS

Main Color - Make 2

Rnd 1- 6 sc in a magic ring

Rnd 2- 6 sc inc(12 sc)

Rnd 3-6- (4 ring)sc into sc (12 sc)

Rnd 7- Only in flo sc into sc(12 sc)

B Color

Rnd 8-22- (15 ring)sc into sc(12 sc)

Rnd 23- Flatten the needle in both layers.

6 sc fo. Do not fill the sleeves.

Arms Detail - Only in blo sc into 3 ch fo.

LEGS AND BODY

Main Color - Make 2

Rnd 1- 6 sc in a magic ring

Rnd 2- 6 sc inc(12 sc)

Rnd 3- (6 times)1 sc into sc next inc(18 sc)

Rnd 4- sc into sc (18 sc)

Rnd 5- 6 sc into sc(6 sc inc)6 sc into sc(24 sc)

Rnd 6- (2 times)sc into sc(24 sc)

Rnd 8- 9 sc into sc(6 sc dec)9 sc into sc(18 sc)

Rnd 9- 8 sc into sc(2 sc dec)8 sc into sc(16 sc)

Rnd 10-23- (14 ring)sc into sc(16 sc)

Stuff the legs tightly. Bring the legs together. Make 4 ch in between.

Rnd 24- 16 sc into sc(4 ch into 4 sc)16 sc into sc(36 sc)

Rnd 25- 4 sc into unworked loops of ch 36 sc into sc(40 sc)

Rnd 26-28- (3 ring)sc into sc(40 sc)

B Color

Rnd 29- Only in flo sc into sc (40 sc)

Rnd 30-32- (3 ring)sc into sc(40 sc)

Rnd 33- Only in flo sc into sc(40 sc)

Rnd 34-36- (3 ring)sc into sc(40 sc)

Rnd 37- Only in flo sc into sc(40 sc)

Rnd 38-44- (7 ring)sc into sc(40 sc)

Rnd 45- (6 times)5 sc into sc next dec(34 sc)

Rnd 46- sc into sc (34 sc)

Rnd 47- (4 times)7 sc into sc next dec(30 sc)

Tightly fill the hull. Keep filling as you go.

Rnd 48- Only in flo sc into sc(30 sc)

Rnd 49- sc into sc(30 sc)fo.

Leave a long thread for sewing.

Elbise detayı- Etek - C Color

Rnd 29- Only in blo sc into 3 cr(120 cr)

Rnd-2- Cr into cr(120 cr)

E Color

Rnd 33- Only in blo sc into 3 cr(120 cr)

Rnd 2- Cr into cr(120 cr)

D Color

Rnd 37- Only in blo sc into 3 cr(120 cr)

Rnd 2- Cr into cr(120 cr)Fo.

Collar Detail - Rnd 48- Only in blo sc into 3 ch fo.

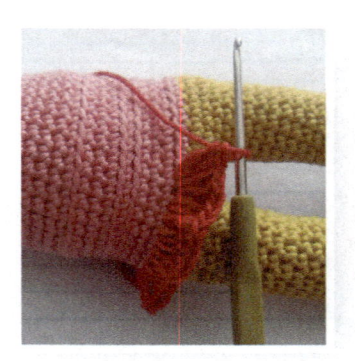

EARS

F COLOR - MAKE 2

Rnd 1- 6 sc in a magic ring

Rnd 2- 6 sc inc(12 sc)

Rnd 3- (6 times)1 sc into sc next inc(18 sc)

Rnd 4- (6 times)2 sc into sc next inc(24 sc)

Rnd 5- (6 times)3 sc into sc next inc(30 sc)

Rnd 6-10- (5 ring)sc into sc(30 sc)

Rnd 11- (6 times)3 sc into sc next dec(24 sc)

Rnd 12-15- (4 ring)sc into sc (24 sc)

Rnd 16- (6 times)2 sc into sc next dec(18 sc)

Rnd 17-21- (5 ring)sc into sc(18 sc)

Rnd 22- Flatten the needle in both layers. 9 sc fo.

Leave a long thread for sewing.

QUEUE

F Color

Rnd 1- 6 sc in a magic ring

Rnd 2- 6 sc inc(12 sc)

Rnd 3- (3 times)3 sc into sc next inc(15 sc)

Rnd 4-6- (3 ring)sc into sc(15 sc)

Rnd 7- (3 times)3 sc into sc next dec(12 sc)

Rnd 8-12 (5 ring)sc into sc(12 sc)

Rnd 13- (4 times)1 sc into sc next dec(8 sc)

Rnd 14-15- (2 ring)sc into sc(8 sc)

Rnd 16- Flatten the needle in both layers. 4 sc fo.

HAIRPINS

C Color - Make 2

20 ch.20 ch into 20 cr

Rnd 2- Turn cr into cr(20 cr)fo.

Wrap the middle of the fold and

Leave a long thread to sew.

Joining of Parts

Sew the ears to both sides Rnd-8.

Sew the sleeves to both sides Rnd-47.

Sew the buckles Rnd-6 to both sides.

NOSE and NOSE TIP

NOSE TIP - F Color

Rnd 1- 2 ch into 2 sc turn

Rnd 2- 1 sc inc 2 sc into sc (3 sc)turn

Rnd 3- 1 sc inc 3 sc into sc(4 sc)turn

Rnd 4- 1 sc inc 4 sc into sc(5 sc)turn

Rnd 5- 1 sc inc 5 sc into sc(6 sc)fo.

Leave a long thread for sewing.

NOSE - A color

Rnd 1- 5 ch ch into sc(10 sc)

Rnd 2- 1 sc inc 4 sc into sc 1 sc inc(12 sc)

Rnd 3- 1 sc inc 5 sc into sc 1 sc inc (14 sc)

Rnd 4- 1 sc inc 6 sc into sc 1 sc inc(16 sc)

Rnd 5- 1 sc inc 7 sc into sc 1 sc inc(18 sc)fo.

Fill the nose, leave a long thread for sewing.

Sew the nose between the 2 eyes between Rnd 16-20. fo.

INSTAGRAM/SEVDATOYSS

Abbreviation/US terminology   :

blo	-	back loop
ch	-	chain
cr	-	crochet
dc	-	double crochet
dc3tog	-	double crochet three together
dec	-	decrease
flo	-	front loop
hdc	-	half double crochet
FO	-	Fasten Off
inc	-	increase
rnd(s)	-	round(s)
sc	-	single crochet
sc3tog	-	single crochet three together
slst	-	slip stitch
st	-	stitch
tr	-	treble stitch
(...)	-	number in parentheses indicates the number of stitches at the end of the round
[...]	-	repeat instructions x times or to the end of the round
(...)	-	work the stitches all into the same stitch

You are welcome to sell items made from this pattern. I would be happy if you link back to my shop and give credit to me as the designer.

Materials:

- Yarn
- 2.5 mm hook size or a size that fits your yarn
- Scissors, stuffing, tapestry needle, stitch marker and pins

Main Color: White **A:** Blue **B:** Fushcia **C:** Red

FINISHED SIZE
Around 15 cm in circumference, about 7 cm in length.

INSTAGRAM/SEVDATOYSS

LEGS & BODY

MAIN COLOR

Rnd 1-6 sc in a mr

Rnd 2-6 sc inc(12)

Rnd 3-(6 times)1 sc into sc next inc(18)

Rnd 4-6-(3 ring)sc into sc(18)

Rnd 7-4 sc into sc(4 sc dec)4 sc into sc(14)

Rnd 8-5 sc into sc (2 sc dec)5 sc into sc(12)

Rnd 9-11-(3 ring)sc into sc(12)

Assemble and stuff the legs.

Rnd 12-sc into sc(24)

Rnd 13-(6 times)3 sc into sc next inc(30)

Rnd 14-sc into sc(30)

Rnd 15-(6 times)4 sc into sc next inc(36)

Rnd 16-20-(5 ring)sc into sc(36)

Rnd 21-(6 times)4 sc into sc next dec(30)

Stuff the body tightly. Keep filling as you go.

Rnd 22-sc into sc(30)

Rnd 23-(6 times)3 sc into sc next dec(24)

Rnd 24-sc into sc(24)

Rnd 25-(6 times)2 sc into sc next dec(18)

Rnd 26-sc into sc(18)

Rnd 27-(6 times)1 sc into sc next dec(12)

Rnd 28-31-(4 ring)sc into sc(12)fo.

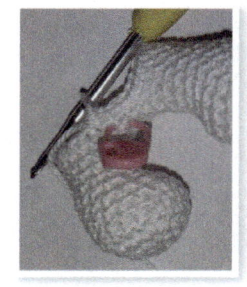

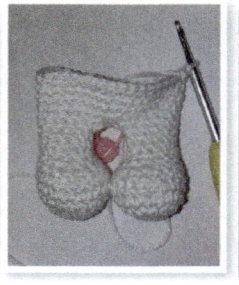

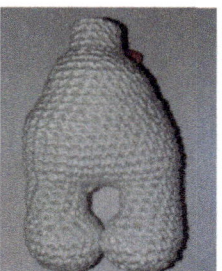

HEAD

MAIN COLOR

Rnd 1-8 sc in a mr

Rnd 2-8 sc inc(16)

Rnd 3-(8 times)1 sc into sc next inc(24)

Rnd 4-(8 times)2 sc into sc next inc(32)

Rnd 5-(8 times)3 sc into sc next inc(40)

Rnd 6-(8 times)4 sc into sc next inc(48)

Rnd 7-11-(5 ring)sc into sc(48)

Rnd 12-(6 times)7 sc into sc next inc(54)

Rnd 13-15-(3 ring)sc into sc(54)

Rnd 16-(6 times)8 sc into sc next inc(60)

Rnd 17-(6 times)8 sc into sc next dec(54)

Rnd 18-3 sc into sc(5 times)7 sc into sc next dec 4 sc into sc(48)

Rnd 19-(6 times)6 sc into sc next dec(42)

Rnd 20-2 sc into sc(5 times)5 sc into sc next dec 3 sc into sc(36)

Rnd 21-(6 times)4 sc into sc next dec(30)

Stuff the head tightly. Keep filling as you go. Place the safe eyes between

rnd 13-14. There should be 9 sc between them.

Rnd 22-1 sc into sc(5 times)3 sc into sc next dec 2 sc into sc(24)

Rnd 23-(8 times)1 sc into sc next dec(16)fo.Leave a long thread end to sew

HAT

A COLOR

Rnd 1-6 sc in a mr

Rnd 2-6 sc inc(12)

Rnd 3-(6 times)1 sc into sc next inc(18)

Rnd 4-(6 times)2 sc into sc next inc(24)

Rnd 5-(6 times)3 sc into sc next inc(30)

Rnd 6-(6 times)4 sc into sc next inc(36)

Rnd 7-(6 times)5 sc into sc next inc(42)

Rnd 8-(6 times)6 sc into sc next inc(48)

Rnd 9-14-(6 ring)sc into sc(48)

Rnd 15-sc into hdc(48 hdc)fo.

ARMS

MAIN COLOR

Rnd 1-6 sc in a mr

Rnd 2-6 sc inc(12)

Rnd 3- 15-(13 ring)sc into sc(12)

Fill the arms a little

Rnd 16-Straighten it. Dip the awl into both layers. 6 sc fo. Leave a long thread to sew on.

EARS - MAKE 2

Rnd 1-6 sc in a mr

Rnd 2-6 sc inc(12)

Rnd 3-sc into sc(12)

Rnd 4-2 sc inc(14)

Rnd 5-sc into sc(14)

Rnd 6-2 sc inc(16)

Rnd 7-sc into sc(16)

Rnd 8-2 sc inc(18)

Rnd 9-sc into sc(18)

Rnd 10-2 sc inc(20)

Rnd 11-sc into sc(20)

Rnd 12-2 sc inc(22)

Rnd 13-14(2 ring)sc into sc(22)

Rnd 15-(4 times)3 sc into sc next dec(18)

Rnd 16-(4 times)2 sc into sc next dec(14)

Rnd 17-Straighten it. Dip the awl into both layers. 7 sc fo. Leave a long thread to sew on.

BASKET

A COLOR

Rnd 1-6 sc in a mr

Rnd 2-6 sc inc(12)

Rnd 3-(6 times)1 sc into sc next inc(18)

Rnd 4-(6 times)2 sc into sc next inc(24)

Rnd 5-İn flo sc into sc(24)

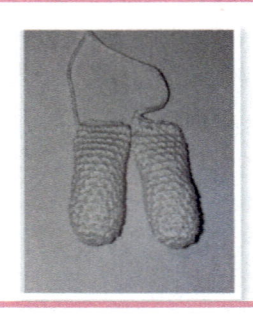

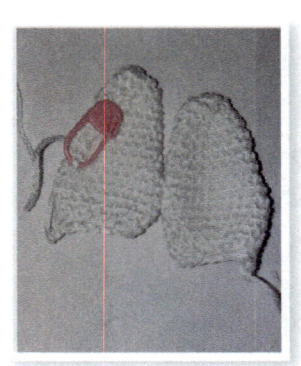

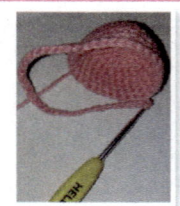

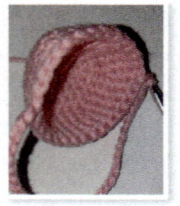

Rnd 6-(6 times)3 sc into sc next inc(30)

Rnd 7-10-(4 ring)sc into sc(30)

Rnd 11-30 ch.

EGG

A COLOR

Rnd 1-6 sc in a mr

Rnd 2-6 sc inc(12)

Rnd 3-2 sc inc(14)

Rnd 4-2 sc inc(16)

Rnd 5-2 sc inc(18)

Rnd 6-2 sc inc(20)

Rnd 7-2 sc inc(22)

Rnd 8-2 sc inc(24)

Rnd 9-12-(4 ring)sc into sc(24) Tightly fill the egg

Rnd 13-(6 times)2 sc into sc next dec(18)

Rnd 14-(6 times)1 sc into sc next dec(12)

Rnd 15-6 sc dec(6)fo.

FLOWER

B COLOR

Rnd 1-10 sc in a mr

Rnd 2-(5 times)1 sc into 3 cr 1 sc into sc fo. Leave a long thread end to sew.

Leaf -C color-

Rnd 1-(2 times)10 ch turn 10 ch into 10 hdc fo.Leave a long thread end to sew.

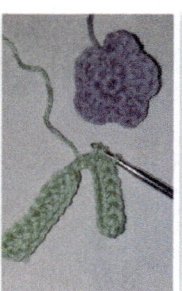

SHORT

B COLOR MAKE 2

Rnd 1-21 ch. Combine.

Rnd 2-4-(3 ring)ch into sc(20 sc) Combine.

Rnd 5-sc into sc(40)

Rnd 6-8-(3 ring)sc into sc(40)

Rnd 9-(8 times)3 sc into sc next dec(32)

Rnd 10-11(2 ring)sc into sc(32)

Rnd 12-3 sc into sc 20 ch.Turn

Rnd 13-ch into sc(20 sc)fo.

JOINING PARTS

Sew sleeves to both sides, rnd-27.

Sew the ears on both sides, on top of the hat to rnd-3.

Sew flowers and leaves to the top of the hat.

FINAL PHOTOS

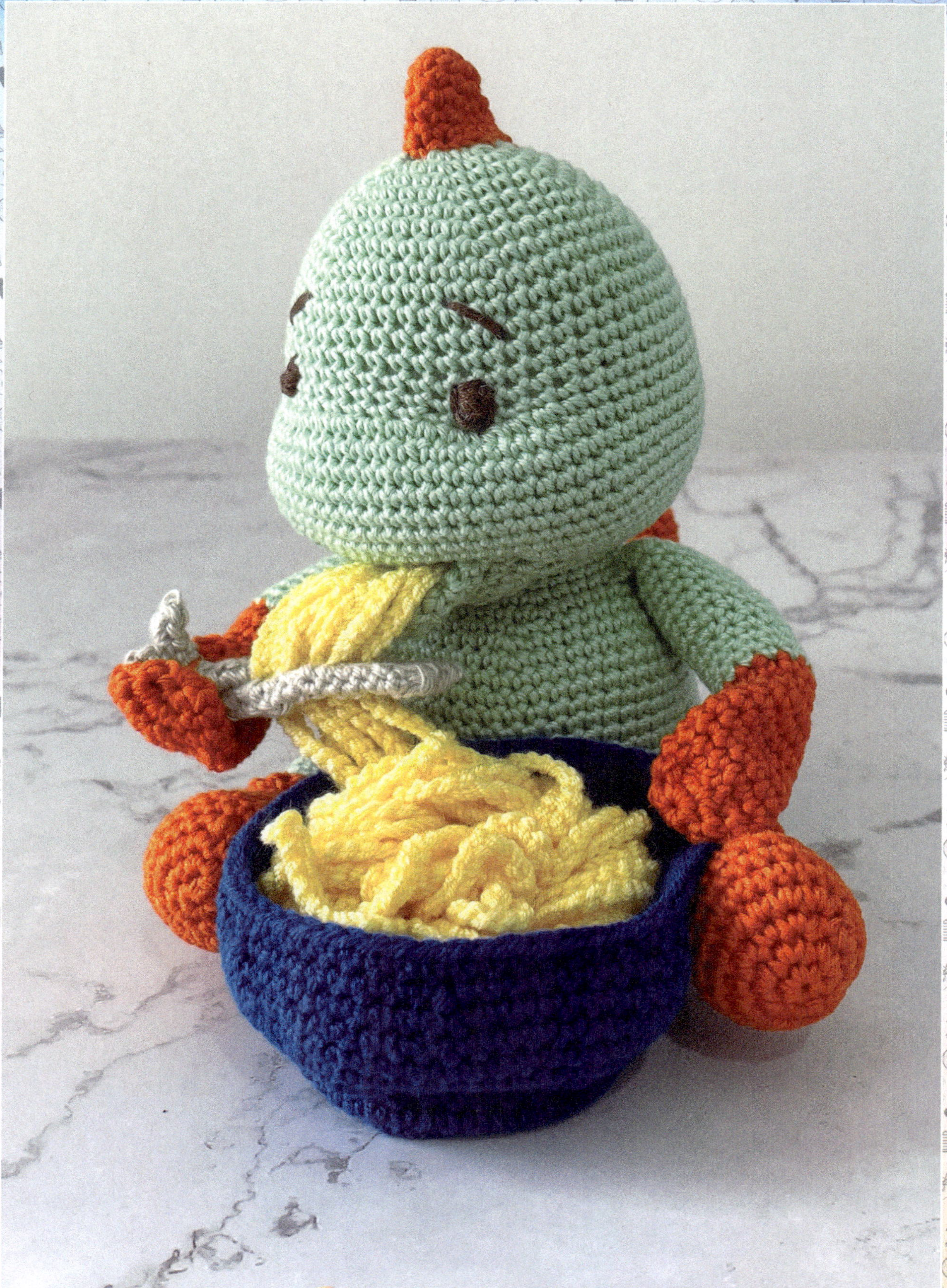

INSTAGRAM/SEVDATOYSS

Abbreviation/US terminology :

blo	-	back loop
ch	-	chain
cr	-	crochet
dc	-	double crochet
dc3tog	-	double crochet three together
dec	-	decrease
flo	-	front loop
hdc	-	half double crochet
FO	-	Fasten Off
inc	-	increase
rnd(s)	-	round(s)
sc	-	single crochet
sc3tog	-	single crochet three together
slst	-	slip stitch
st	-	stitch
tr	-	treble stitch
(...)	-	number in parentheses indicates the number of stitches at the end of the round
[...]	-	repeat instructions x times or to the end of the round
(...)	-	work the stitches all into the same stitch

You are welcome to sell items made from this pattern. I would be happy if you link back to my shop and give credit to me as the designer.

Materials:

- Yarn
- 2.5 mm hook size or a size that fits your yarn
- Scissors, stuffing, tapestry needle, stitch marker and pins

Main Color: Green **A:** Blue **B:** Orange **C:** Yellow

FINISHED SIZE
Around 20 cm in circumference, about 10 cm in length.

HEAD & BODY

MAIN COLOR

Rnd 1-6 sc in a mr

Rnd 2-6 sc inc(12)

Rnd 3-(6 times)1 sc into sc next inc(18)

Rnd 4-(6 times)2 sc into sc next inc(24)

Rnd 5-(6 times)3 sc into sc next inc(30)

Rnd 6-(6 times)4 sc into sc next inc(36)

Rnd 7-(6 times)5 sc into sc next inc(42)

Rnd 8-(6 times)6 sc into sc next inc(48)

Rnd 9-(6 times)7 sc into sc next inc(54)

Rnd 10-15-(6 ring)sc into sc(54)

Rnd 16-20 sc into sc(14 sc inc)20 sc into sc(68)

Rnd 17-23-(7 ring)sc into sc(68)

Rnd 24-20 sc into sc(14 sc dec)20 sc into sc(54)

Rnd 25-(6 times)7 sc into sc next dec(48)

Rnd 26-(6 times)6 sc into sc next dec(42)

Rnd 27-(6 times)5 sc into sc next dec(36)

Rnd 28-(6 times)4 sc into sc next dec(30)

Tightly fill the head

Rnd 29-31-(3 ring)sc into sc(30)

Rnd 32-(6 times)4 sc into sc next inc(36)

Rnd 33-(6 times)5 sc into sc next inc(42)

Rnd 34-(6 times)6 sc into sc next inc(48)

Rnd 35-(6 times)7 sc into sc next inc(54)

Rnd 36-43-(8 ring)sc into sc(54)

B COLOR

Rnd 44-İn flo sc into sc(54)

Rnd 45-58-(14 ring)sc into sc (54)

Rnd 59-İn flo sc into sc(54)

Rnd 60-(6 times)7 sc into sc next dec(48)

Rnd 61-(6 times)6 sc into sc next dec(42)

Rnd 62-(6 times)5 sc into sc next dec(36)

Rnd 63-(6 times)4 sc into sc next dec(30)

Rnd 64-(6 times)3 sc into sc next dec(24)

Rnd 65-(6 times)2 sc into sc next dec(18)

Rnd 66-(6 times)1 sc into sc next dec(12)

Rnd 67-6 sc dec fo.

LOWER LIP - MAIN COLOR

Rnd 1-6 sc in a mr

Rnd2-6 sc inc(12)

Rnd 3-sc into sc(12)

Rnd 4-(6 times)1 sc into sc next inc(18)

Rnd 5-sc into sc (18)

Rnd 6-(6 times)2 sc into sc next inc(24)

Rnd 7-sc into sc(24)

Rnd 8-Straighten it. Dip the awl into both layers. 12 sc fo. Leave a long thread end to sew.

TAIL

MAIN COLOR

Rnd 1-6 sc in a mr

Rnd 2-sc into sc(6)

Rnd 3-2 sc inc(8)

Rnd 4-sc into sc(8)

Rnd 5-2 sc inc(10)

Rnd 6-sc into sc(10)

Rnd 7-2 sc inc(12)

Rnd 8-sc into sc(12)

Rnd 9-(6 times)1 sc into sc next inc(18)

Rnd 10-16-(7 ring)sc into sc(18)

Rnd 17-(2 times)8 sc into sc next inc(20)

Rnd 18(2 times)9 sc into sc next inc(22)

Rnd 19-sc into sc(22)

Rnd 20-(2 times)10 sc into sc next inc(24)

Rnd 21-sc into sc(24) Tightly fill the tail

Rnd 22-(6 times)4 sc into sc next inc(30)

Rnd 23-24-(2 ring)sc into sc(30)fo.Leave a long thread end to sew.

ARMS

B COLOR - MAKE 2

Rnd 1-6 sc in a mr

Rnd 2-6 sc inc(12)

Rnd 3-sc into sc(12)

Rnd 4-2 sc inc(14)

Rnd 5-8-(4 ring)sc into sc(14)

Rnd 9-(4 times)2 sc into sc next dec(10)

Rnd 10-sc into sc(10)

Rnd 11-(5 times)1 sc into sc next inc(15)

Ana color-

Rnd 12-23-(12 ring)sc into sc(15)

Rnd 24-Straighten it. Dip the awl into both layers. 7 sc fo. Leave a long thread end to sew.

LEGS

MAKE 2 - B COLOR

Rnd 1-6 sc in a mr

Rnd 2-6 sc inc(12)

Rnd 3-(6 times)1 sc into sc next inc(18)

Rnd 4-6 sc into sc(4 sc inc)6 sc into sc(22)

Rnd 5-7-(3 ring)sc into sc(22) Tightly fill the legs

Rnd 8-6 sc into sc(4 sc dec)6 sc into sc(18)

Rnd 9-7 sc into sc(2 sc dec)7 sc into sc(16)

Rnd 10-11-(2 ring)sc into sc(16)

Rnd 12-İn flo sc into sc(16) MAIN COLOR

Rnd 13-20-(8 ring)sc into sc(16)

Rnd 21-Straighten it. Dip the awl into both layers. 8 sc fo. Leave a long thread end to sew.

LEG DETAILS-Rnd 12-İn blo sc into sc(16)fo.clean the thread end.

SPAGHETTI BOWL

A COLOR

Rnd 1-6 sc in a mr

Rnd 2-6 sc inc(12)

Rnd 3-(6 times)1 sc into sc next inc(18)

Rnd 4-(6 times)2 sc into sc next inc(24)

Rnd5-(6 times)3 sc into sc next inc(30)

Rnd 6-(6 times)4 sc into sc next inc(36)

Rnd 6-(6 times)5 sc into sc next inc(42)

Rnd 8-İn flo sc into sc(42)

Rnd 9-10-(2 ring)sc into sc(42)

Rnd 11-İn blo (6 times)6 sc into sc next inc(48)

Rnd 12-(6 times)7 sc into sc next inc(54)

Rnd 13-(6 times)8 sc into sc next inc(60)

Rnd 14-16-(3 ring)sc into sc(60)

Rnd 17-(6 times)7 sc into sc next dec(54)fo..

DINOSAUR BACK

B COLOR

Rnd 1-6 sc in a mr

Rnd 2-2 sc inc(8)

Rnd 3-2 sc inc(10)

Rnd 4-2 sc inc(12)

Rnd 5-6-(2 ring)sc into sc(12)fo.Leave a long thread end to sew.

SPAGHETTIES & STICK

C COLOR - MAKE 7

100 ch.

STICK - LIGHT BROWN

Rnd 1-20 ch turn

Rnd 2-20 ch into sc(40 sc)fo.Fold it up.

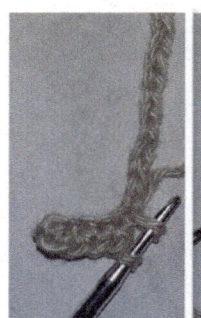

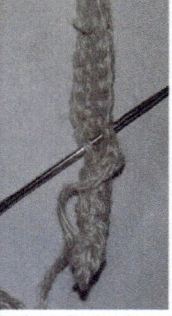

JOINING PARTS

Sew top of 1 sc "6 times" between eyes Rnd 14-15. there should be 8 sc between them.

Sew the tail back.

Sew sleeves to both sides, between rnd 30-33

Sew the legs to both sides, between rnd 55-59.

Sew the back to 2 heads, 2 body and tail ends.

FINAL PHOTOS

INSTAGRAM/SEVDATOYSS

Abbreviation/US terminology :

blo	-	back loop
ch	-	chain
cr	-	crochet
dc	-	double crochet
dc3tog	-	double crochet three together
dec	-	decrease
flo	-	front loop
hdc	-	half double crochet
FO	-	Fasten Off
inc	-	increase
rnd(s)	-	round(s)
sc	-	single crochet
sc3tog	-	single crochet three together
slst	-	slip stitch
st	-	stitch
tr	-	treble stitch
(...)	-	number in parentheses indicates the number of stitches at the end of the round
[...]	-	repeat instructions x times or to the end of the round
(...)	-	work the stitches all into the same stitch

You are welcome to sell items made from this pattern. I would be happy if you link back to my shop and give credit to me as the designer.

Materials:

- Yarn
- 2.5 mm hook size or a size that fits your yarn
- Scissors, stuffing, tapestry needle, stitch marker and pins

Main Color: Dark Blue **A:** White **B:** Orange **C:** Red

FINISHED SIZE
Around 20 cm in circumference, about 10 cm in length.

INSTAGRAM/SEVDATOYSS

HEAD & BODY

MAIN COLOR

Rnd 1-8 sc in a mr

Rnd 2-8 sc inc(16)

Rnd 3-(8 times)1 sc into sc next inc(24)

Rnd 4-(8 times)2 sc into sc next inc(32)

Rnd 5-(8 times)3 sc into sc next inc(40)

Rnd 6-(8 times)4 sc into sc next inc(48)

Rnd 7-(8 times)5 sc into sc next inc(56)

Rnd 8-10 ch turn 10 ch into hdc 1sc into sc again 10 ch.Ch into hdc sc into sc(56)

Rnd 9- Leave strands of hair out. go on. sc into sc (56)

Rnd 10-12-(3 ring)sc into sc(56)

Rnd 13-(8 times)6 sc into sc next inc(64)

Rnd 14-21-(8 ring)sc into sc(64)

Install the safety eyes between rnd 19-20. there should be 11 sc between them

Rnd 22-(8 times)6 sc into sc next dec(56)

Rnd 23-sc into sc(56)

Rnd 24-(8 times)5 sc into sc next dec(48)

Rnd 25-sc into sc(48)

Rnd 26-(8 times)4 sc into sc next dec(40)

Rnd 27-sc into sc(40)

Rnd 28-(8 times)3 sc into sc next dec(32)

Rnd 29-31-(3 ring)sc into sc(32)

Tightly fill the head

Rnd 32-(8 times)3 sc into sc next inc(40)

Rnd 33-sc into sc(40)

Rnd 34-(8 times)4 sc into sc next inc(48)

Rnd 35-(8 times)5 sc into sc next inc(56)

Rnd 36-39-(4 ring)sc into sc(56)

Rnd 40-(8 times)6 sc into sc next inc((64)

Rnd 41-49-(9 ring)sc into sc(64)

Rnd 50-in flo sc into sc(64)Tightly fill the body

Rnd 51-(8 times)6 sc into sc next dec(56)

Rnd 52-(8 times)5 sc into sc next dec(48)

Rnd 53-(8 times)4 sc into sc next dec(40)

Rnd 54-(8 times)3 sc into sc next dec(32)

Rnd 55-(8 times)2 sc into sc next dec(24)

Rnd 56-(8 times)1 sc into sc next dec(16)

Rnd 57-(8 times)1 sc into sc next dec(8)

Rnd 58-(8 times)1 sc into sc next dec(4)fo.

ARMS

MAKE 2 - A COLOR

Rnd 1-6 sc in a mr-

Rnd 2-6 sc inc(12)

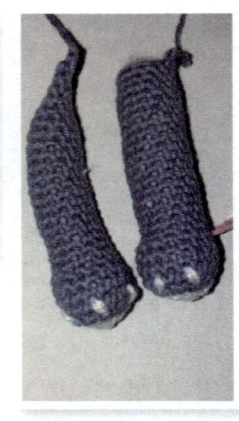

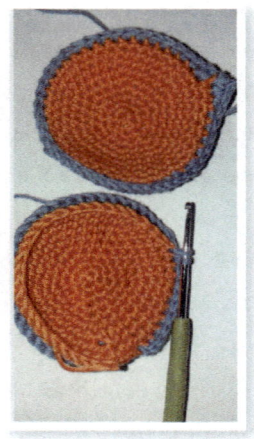

MAIN COLOR

Rnd 3-4 sc into sc(4 sc inc)4 sc into sc(16)

Rnd 4-6-(3 ring)sc into sc(16)

Rnd 7-4 sc into sc(4 sc dec)4 sc into sc(12)

Fill sleeves keep filling as you go

Rnd 8-27-(19 ring)sc into sc(12)

Rnd 28-Straighten it. sink the needle into both layers. 6 sc fo. Leave a long thread to sew on.

Do it by sewing the paws. Repeat the stitch 3 times.

LEGS

MAKE 2 - A COLOR

Rnd 1-6 sc in a mr

Rnd 2-6 sc inc(12) Ana color

Rnd 3-4 sc into sc(4 sc inc)4 sc into sc(16)

Rnd 4-6 sc into sc(4 sc inc)6 sc into sc(20)

Rnd 5-sc into sc(20)

Rnd 6-6 sc into sc(4 sc dec)6 sc into sc(16)

Rnd 7-16-(10 ring)sc into sc(16)

Rnd 17-Straighten it. sink the needle into both layers. (8 sc)fo.

Leave a long thread to sew on.

EARS

MAKE 4 - MAIN COLOR 2 - B COLOR 2

Rnd 1-6 sc in a mr

Rnd 2-6 sc inc(12)

Rnd 3-(6 times)1 sc into sc next inc(18)

Rnd 4-(6 times)2 sc into sc next inc(24)

Rnd 5-(6 times)3 sc into sc next inc(30)

Rnd 6-(6 times)4 sc into sc next inc(36)

Rnd 7-(6 times)5 sc into sc next inc(42)

Rnd 8-9(2 ring)sc into sc (42)

Rnd 10-Combine the main color and A color ears. Knit the edge with the main color yarn. sc into sc(42)fo. a long thread for sewing leave it.

TRUNK

MAIN COLOR

Rnd 1-6 sc in a mr

Rnd 2-(4 times)sc inc(10)

Rnd 3-12-(10 ring)sc into sc(10)

Rnd 13-(2 times) sc inc(12) Fill the elephant's trunk. Keep filling as you go.

Rnd 14-23-(10 ring)sc into sc(12)

Rnd 24-(2 times) sc inc(14)

Rnd 25-31-(7 ring) sc into sc(14)fo.Leave a long thread to sew on.

STOMACH

A COLOR

Rnd 1-6 sc in a mr

Rnd 2-6 sc inc(12)

Rnd 3-(6 times)1 sc into sc next inc(18)

Rnd 4-(6 times)2 sc into sc next inc(24)

Rnd 5-(6 times)3 sc into sc next inc(30)

Rnd 6-(6 times)4 sc into sc next inc(36)

Rnd 7-(6 times)5 sc into sc next inc(42)

Rnd 8-(6 times)6 sc into sc next inc(48)fo.Leave a long thread to sew on.

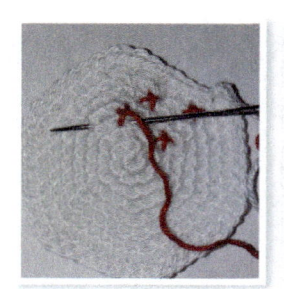

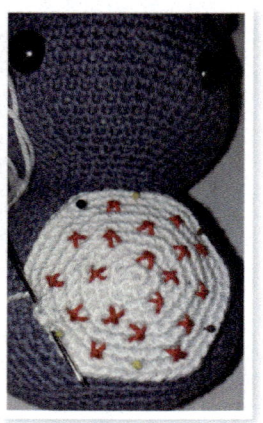

TAIL

A COLOR

Rnd 1-6 sc in a mr

Rnd 2-2 sc inc(8)

Ana color

Rnd 3-(4 times)1 sc into sc next inc(12)

Rnd 4-8-(5 ring)sc into sc(12)

Rnd 9-2 sc dec(10)Fill the tail. keep filling as you go

Rnd 10-23-(14 ring)sc into sc(10)

Rnd 24-Straighten it. sink the needle into both layers 5 sc fo. Leave a long thread to sew on.

SCARF

Rnd 1-80 ch.

Rnd 2-80 ch into sc(80 sc)fo.

JOINING PARTS

Sew the ears on both sides between Rnd 10-17. There should be 18 sc between them.

Sleeves- Sew between first sleeve rnd 37-42. Lift second arm up and sew between rnd 37-42.

Sew the legs on both sides between rnd 44-51.

Sew the hose in the middle of the two eyes between rnd 15-20.

Mark the middle of the body with the tail back. Sew between rnd 48-51.

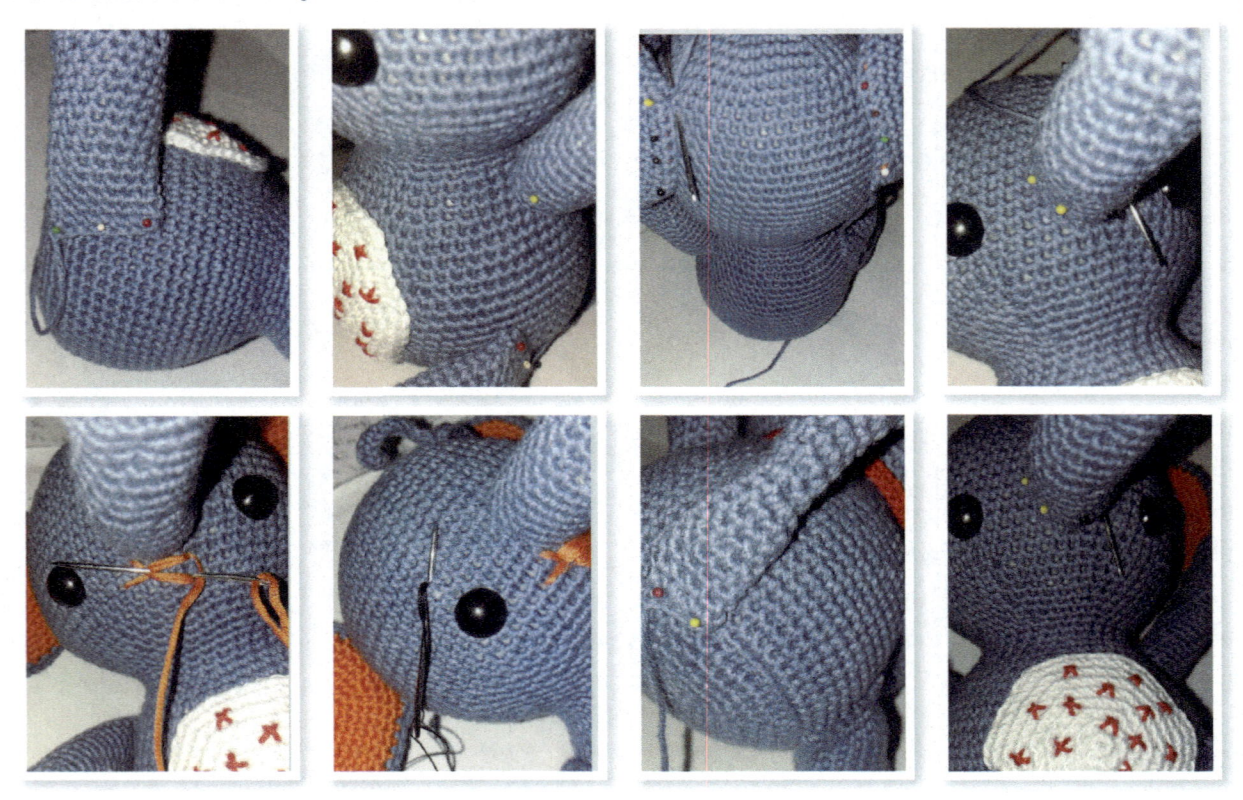

FINAL PHOTOS

ARMS

MAKE 2 - A COLOR

Rnd 1-6 sc in a mr-

Rnd 2-6 sc inc(12)

MAIN COLOR

Rnd 3-4 sc into sc(4 sc inc)4 sc into sc(16)

Rnd 4-6-(3 ring)sc into sc(16)

Rnd 7-4 sc into sc(4 sc dec)4 sc into sc(12)

Fill sleeves keep filling as you go

Rnd 8-27-(19 ring)sc into sc(12)

Rnd 28-Straighten it. sink the needle into both layers. 6 sc fo. Leave a long thread to sew on.

Do it by sewing the paws. Repeat the stitch 3 times.

LEGS

MAKE 2 - A COLOR

Rnd 1-6 sc in a mr

Rnd 2-6 sc inc(12) Ana color

Rnd 3-4 sc into sc(4 sc inc)4 sc into sc(16)

Rnd 4-6 sc into sc(4 sc inc)6 sc into sc(20)

Rnd 5-sc into sc(20)

Rnd 6-6 sc into sc(4 sc dec)6 sc into sc(16)

Rnd 7-16-(10 ring)sc into sc(16)

Rnd 17-Straighten it. sink the needle into both layers. (8 sc)fo.

Leave a long thread to sew on.

EARS

MAKE 4 - MAIN COLOR 2 - B COLOR 2

Rnd 1-6 sc in a mr

Rnd 2-6 sc inc(12)

Rnd 3-(6 times)1 sc into sc next inc(18)

Rnd 4-(6 times)2 sc into sc next inc(24)

Rnd 5-(6 times)3 sc into sc next inc(30)

Rnd 6-(6 times)4 sc into sc next inc(36)

Rnd 7-(6 times)5 sc into sc next inc(42)

Rnd 8-9(2 ring)sc into sc (42)

Rnd 10-Combine the main color and A color ears. Knit the edge with the main color yarn. sc into sc(42)fo. a long thread for sewing leave it.

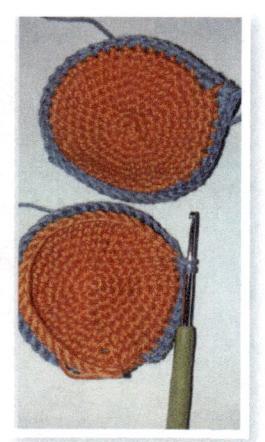

INSTAGRAM/SEVDATOYSS

Abbreviation/US terminology :

blo	-	back loop
ch	-	chain
cr	-	crochet
dc	-	double crochet
dc3tog	-	double crochet three together
dec	-	decrease
flo	-	front loop
hdc	-	half double crochet
FO	-	Fasten Off
inc	-	increase
rnd(s)	-	round(s)
sc	-	single crochet
sc3tog	-	single crochet three together
slst	-	slip stitch
st	-	stitch
tr	-	treble stitch
(...)	-	number in parentheses indicates the number of stitches at the end of the round
[...]	-	repeat instructions x times or to the end of the round
(...)	-	work the stitches all into the same stitch

You are welcome to sell items made from this pattern. I would be happy if you link back to my shop and give credit to me as the designer.

Materials:

- Yarn
- 2.5 mm hook size or a size that fits your yarn
- Scissors, stuffing, tapestry needle, stitch marker and pins

Main Color: Dark Cream Clear **A:** Green **B:** White **C:** Yellow **D:** Dark Green **E:** Orange

FINISHED SIZE
Around 20 cm in circumference, about 10 cm in length.

HEAD

MAIN COLOR

Rnd 1-6 sc in a mr

Rnd 2-6 sc inc(12 sc)

Rnd 3-1 sc into sc next inc(18)

Rnd 4-2 sc into sc next inc(24)

Rnd 5-3 sc into sc next inc(30)

Rnd 6-4 sc into sc next inc(36)

Rnd 7-5 sc into sc next inc(42)

Rnd 8-6 sc into sc next inc(48)

Rnd 9-7 sc into sc next inc(54)

Rnd 10-20-(11 ring)sc into sc(54 sc)

Rnd 21-15 sc into sc(9 sc inc)6 sc into sc(9 sc inc)15 sc into sc(72 sc)

Rnd 22-27-(6 ring)sc into sc(72 sc)

Rnd 28-(6 times)10 sc into sc next dec(66)

Rnd 29-(6 times)9 sc into sc next dec(60)

Rnd 30-(6 times)8 sc into sc next dec(54)

Rnd 31-(6 times)7 sc into sc next dec(48)

Rnd 32-(6 times)6 sc into sc next dec(42)

Place the safety eyes between rnd 18 and 19. There will be 8 sc between them.

Rnd 33-(6 times)5 sc into sc next dec(36)

Stuff the head tightly. Keep filling as you go.

Rnd 34-(6 times)4 sc into sc next dec(30)

Rnd 35-(6 times)3 sc into sc next dec(24)

Rnd 36-(6 times)2 sc into sc next dec(18)fo. Leave a long thread to sew on.

EARS AND NOSE

EARS - MAKE 2, MAIN COLOR

Rnd 1-6 sc in a mr

Rnd 2-6 sc inc(12)

Rnd 3-1 sc into sc next inc(18)

Rnd 3-2 sc into sc next inc(24)

Rnd 4-3 sc into sc next inc(30)

Rnd 5-4 sc into sc next inc(36)

Rnd 6-9-(4 ring)sc into sc(36 sc)fo.Leave a long thread to sew on.

NOSE - MAIN COLOR

Rnd 1-6 sc in a mr

Rnd 2-6 sc inc(12)

Rnd 3-(6 times)1 sc into sc next inc(18)

Rnd 4-sc into sc(18)

Rnd 5-(6 times)2 sc into sc next inc(24)

Rnd 6-sc into sc(24 sc)fo.Leave a long thread to sew on.

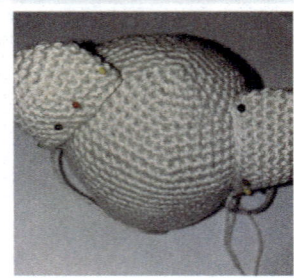

LEGS

Rnd 1-6 sc in a mr

Rnd 2-6 sc inc(12)

Rnd 3-(6 times)1 sc into sc next inc(18)

Rnd 4-6 sc into sc(6 sc inc)6 sc into sc(24)

Rnd 5-7-(3 ring)sc into sc(24 sc)

Rnd 8-6 sc into sc (6 sc dec)6 sc into sc(18)

Rnd 9-5 sc into sc(4 sc dec)5 sc into sc(14)

Rnd 10-15-(6 ring)sc into sc(14)

Rnd 16-A color-sc into sc(14)

Rnd 17-İn flo sc into sc(14)

Rnd 18-14 sc inc(28)

Rnd 19-25-(7 ring)sc into sc(28)

Rnd 26-join the legs sc into sc(56 sc)

Rnd 27-33-(7 ring)sc into sc(56 sc)

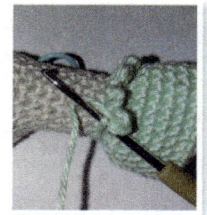

Rnd 34-(8 times)6 sc into sc next dec(48)

Rnd 35-(6 times)6 sc into sc next dec(42)

Rnd 36-Main color-sc into sc(42)

Rnd 37-(6 times)5 sc into sc next dec(36)

Rnd 38-39-(2 ring)sc into sc(36)

Rnd 40-(6 times)4 sc into sc next dec(30)

Rnd 41-42-(2 ring)sc into sc(30)

Stuff the body tightly. Keep filling as you go.

Rnd 43-(6 times)3 sc into sc next dec(24)

Rnd 44-sc into sc (24)

Rnd 45-(6 times)2 sc into sc next dec(18)

Rnd 46-sc into sc(18)fo.

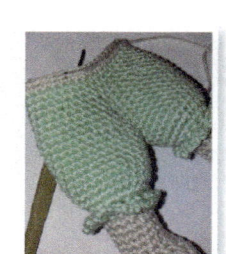

DRESS

A COLOR

Rnd 1-32 ch.Turn

Rnd 2-32 ch into sc(32 sc)1 ch turn

Rnd 3-sc into sc (32 sc)1 ch turn

Rnd 4-1 sc into sc next inc(48 sc)1 ch turn

Rnd 5-sc into sc(48)6 ch .rnd 1 sink in.. turn 6 ch into 6 sc

Rnd 6-10 sc into sc 10 ch (6 sc skip)16 sc into sc(6 sc skip)10 sc into sc(48 sc)

Rnd 7-10 sc into sc(10 ch into sc)16 sc into sc(10 ch into sc)10 sc into sc(56 sc)

Rnd 8- Combine. 56 sc into cr(56 cr)

Rnd 9-13-(5 ring)cr into cr(56 cr)

Rnd 14-56 cr inc(112 cr)

Rnd 15-112 cr into 4 ch fo.

Arms Detail - 10 sc into ch.fo.

ARMS

MAIN COLOR - MAKE 2

Rnd 1-6 sc in a mr

Rnd 2-6 sc inc(12)

Rnd 3-19-(17 ring)sc into sc(12)

Rnd 20- Straighten it. Dip the awl into both layers. 6 sc fo. Leave a long thread end to sew.

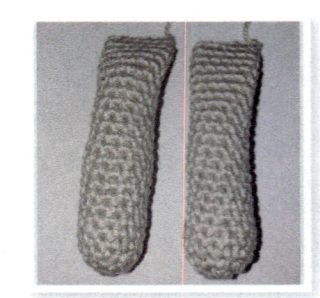

BASKET

D COLOR

Rnd 1-8 sc in a mr

Rnd 2-8 sc inc(16)

Rnd 3-1 sc into sc next inc(24)

Rnd 4-2 sc into sc next inc(32)

Rnd 5-3 sc into sc next inc(40)

Rnd 6-in flo sc into sc(40)

Rnd 7-11-(5 ring)sc into sc(40)

Rnd 12-20 ch.20 ch into sc(20 sc)fo.

MUSHROOMS

Rnd 1-6 sc in a mr

Rnd 2-6 sc inc(12)

Rnd 3-1 sc into sc next inc(18)

Rnd 4-sc into sc(18)

Rnd 5-2 sc into sc next inc(24)

Rnd 6-İn flo sc into sc(24)

Rnd 7-1 sc into sc next dec(12)

B color-sc into sc(12)

Stuff the mushroom. Keep filling as you go.

Rnd 8-12(5 ring)sc into sc(12)

Rnd 13-1 sc into sc next dec(6)fo. Leave a long thread. Make spots of the mushroom with that thread.

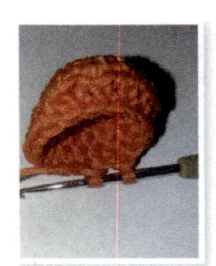

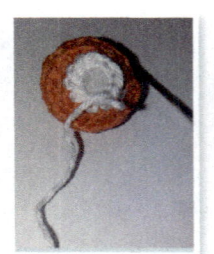

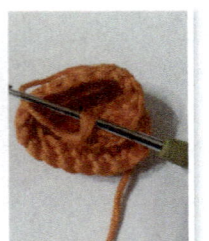

CROWN FLOWER

Rnd 1-10 sc in a mr

Rnd 2-B color-(5 times)1 sc into 5 cr (5 times)1 sc into sc

Belt -A color- 130 ch.130 ch into sc(130 sc)fo.

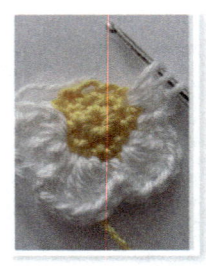

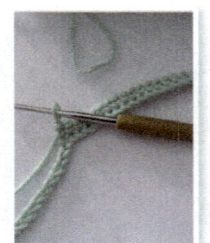

FINAL PHOTOS

51

INSTAGRAM/SEVDATOYSS

Abbreviation/US terminology :

blo	-	back loop
ch	-	chain
cr	-	crochet
dc	-	double crochet
dc3tog	-	double crochet three together
dec	-	decrease
flo	-	front loop
hdc	-	half double crochet
FO	-	Fasten Off
inc	-	increase
rnd(s)	-	round(s)
sc	-	single crochet
sc3tog	-	single crochet three together
slst	-	slip stitch
st	-	stitch
tr	-	treble stitch
(...)	-	number in parentheses indicates the number of stitches at the end of the round
[...]	-	repeat instructions x times or to the end of the round
(...)	-	work the stitches all into the same stitch

You are welcome to sell items made from this pattern. I would be happy if you link back to my shop and give credit to me as the designer.

Materials:

- Yarn
- 2.5 mm hook size or a size that fits your yarn
- Scissors, stuffing, tapestry needle, stitch marker and pins

Main Color: White **A:** Green **B:** Red **C:** Cream

Little light brown and dark brown

FINISHED SIZE
Around 20 cm in circumference, about 10 cm in length.

INSTAGRAM/SEVDATOYSS

BODY

MAIN COLOR

Rnd 1-6 sc in a mr

Rnd 2-6 sc inc(12)

Rnd 3-(6 times)1 sc into sc next inc(18)

Rnd 4-(6 times)2 sc into sc next inc(24)

Rnd 5-(6 times)3 sc into sc next inc(30)

Rnd 6-(6 times)4 sc into sc next inc(36)

Rnd 7-(6 times)5 sc into sc next inc(42)

Rnd 8-(6 times)6 sc into sc next inc(48)

Rnd 9-İn flo sc into sc(48 sc)

Rnd 10-13-(4 ring)sc into sc(48 sc)

Rnd 14-(6 times)6 sc into sc next dec(42)

Rnd 15-16-(2 ring)sc into sc(42 sc)

A color-

Rnd 17-sc into sc(42)

Rnd 18-(6 times)5 sc into sc next dec(36)

Rnd 19-27-(9 ring)sc into sc(36)

Rnd 28-(6 times)4 sc into sc next dec(30 sc)

Stuff the body tightly. Keep filling as you go.

Rnd 29-36-(8 ring)sc into sc(30)

Rnd 37-(6 times)3 sc into sc next dec(24)

Rnd 38-40-(3 ring)sc into sc(24)fo.

HEAD

Rnd 1-6 sc in a mr

Rnd 2-6 sc inc(12)

Rnd 3-(6 times)1 sc into sc next inc(18)

Rnd 4-(6 times)2 sc into sc next inc(24)

Rnd 5-(6 times)3 sc into sc next inc(30)

Rnd 6-(6 times)4 sc into sc next inc(36)

Rnd 7-(6 times)5 sc into sc next inc(42)

Rnd 8-(6 times)6 sc into sc next inc(48)

Rnd 9-(6 times)7 sc into sc next inc(54)

Rnd 10-20-(11 ring)sc into sc(54 sc)

Rnd 21-15 sc into sc(9 sc inc)6 sc into sc(9 sc inc)15 sc into sc(72 sc)

Rnd 22-27-(6 ring)sc into sc(72 sc)

Rnd 28-((6 times)10 sc into sc next dec(66 sc)

Rnd 29-(6 times)9 sc into sc next dec(60 sc)

Rnd 30-(6 times)8 sc into sc next dec(54)

Rnd 31-(6 times)7 sc into sc next dec(48)

Attach the safety eyes to rnd 18-19. There will be 8 sc between them

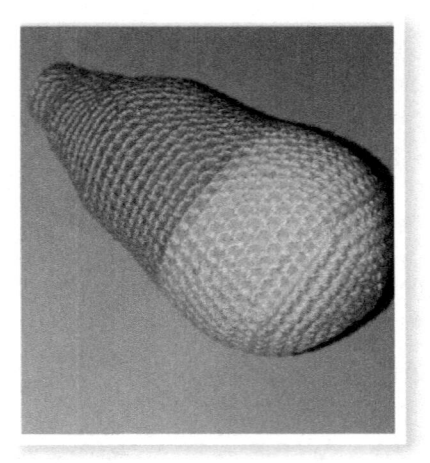

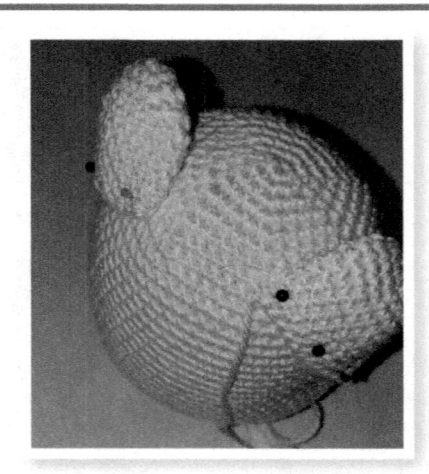

HEAD MORE

Rnd 32-(6 times)6 sc into sc next dec(42)

Rnd 33-(6 times)5 sc into sc next dec(36)

Stuff the head tightly. keep filling as you go

Rnd 34-(6 times)4 sc into sc next dec(30)

Rnd 35-(6 times)3 sc into sc next dec(24)

Rnd 36-sc into sc(24 sc)

Rnd 37-(6 times)2 sc into sc next dec(18)fo.

Leave a long thread to sew on.

NOSE

MAIN COLOR

Rnd 1-6 sc in a mr

Rnd 2-6 sc inc(12)

Rnd 3-(6 times)1 sc into sc next inc(18)

Rnd 4-sc into sc (18)

Rnd 5-(6 times)2 sc into sc next inc(24)

Rnd 6-8-(3 ring)sc into sc (24 sc)fo.

Leave a long thread to sew on.

LEGS

MAIN COLOR - MAKE 2

Rnd 1-6 sc in a mr

Rnd 2-6 sc inc(12)

Rnd 3-(6 times)1 sc into sc next inc(18)

Rnd 4-(6 times)2sc into sc next inc(24)

Rnd 5-(6 times)3 sc into sc next inc(30)

Stuff the legs tightly. keep filling as you go

Rnd 6-11-(6 ring)sc into sc(30 sc)

Rnd 12-10 sc into sc(10 sc dec)10 sc into sc(20 sc)

Rnd 13-25-(13 ring)sc into sc(20 sc)

Rnd 26-Straighten it. Dip the awl into both layers. 10 sc fo.

Leave a long thread to sew on.

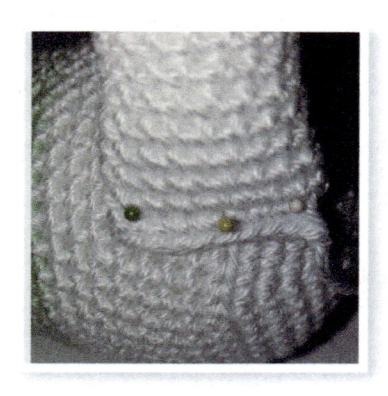

ARMS

MAIN COLOR

Rnd 1-6 sc in a mr

Rnd 2-6 sc inc(12)

Rnd 3-(6 times)1 sc into sc next inc(18)

Rnd 4-(6 times)2 sc into sc next inc(24)

Rnd 5-10-(6 ring)sc into sc (24 sc)

Rnd 11-6 sc into sc(6 sc dec)6 sc into sc(18 sc)

Rnd 12-17-(6 ring)sc into sc(18)

A COLOR -Just fill the end of the arm

Rnd 18-36-(19 ring)sc into sc(18 sc)

Rnd 37-Straighten it. Dip the awl into both layers. 10 sc fo.

Leave a long thread to sew on.

GLASS

C COLOR

Rnd 1-8 sc in a mr

Rnd 2-8 sc inc(16)

Rnd 3-(8 times)1sc into sc next inc(24)

Rnd 4-sc into sc (24)

Rnd 5-İn flo sc intosc(24)

Rnd 6-7-(2 ring)sc into sc (24 sc)

Rnd 8-(8 times)2 sc into sc next inc(32)

Rnd 9-12-(4 ring)sc into sc(32)

Rnd 13-A color-sc into sc(32)

Rnd 14-C color-sc into sc(32)

Rnd 15-B color-(8 times)3 sc into sc next inc(40)

Rnd 16-C color-sc into sc(40)

Rnd 17-A color-sc into sc(40)

Rnd 18-24-C color-(7 ring)sc into sc(40 sc)

Rnd 25-sc into hdc (40 hdc)fo.

THE BOTTOM OF THE GLASS -

Rnd 5-in blo sc into hdc(24 hdc)

COLLAR - B COLOR

Rnd 1-30 ch.30 ch into sc(30 sc)1 ch turn

Rnd 2-30 sc inc cr (60 cr)fo.

EARS

MAIN COLOR

Rnd 1-6 sc in a mr

Rnd 2-6 sc inc(12)

Rnd 3-(6 times)1 sc into sc next inc(18)

Rnd 4-(6 times)1 sc into sc next inc(24)

Rnd 5-11-(7 ring)sc into sc (24 sc)

Rnd 12-Straighten it. Dip the awl into both layers. (12 sc) fo. Leave a long thread to sew on.

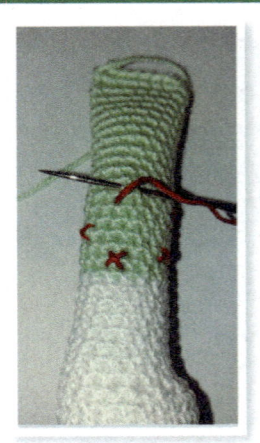

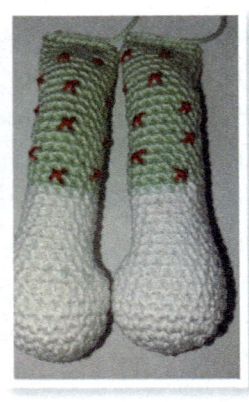

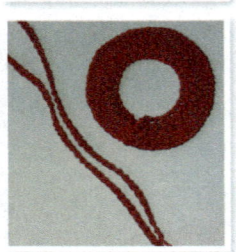

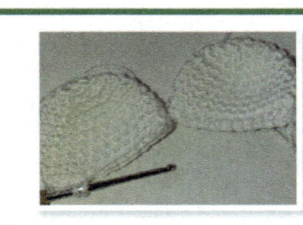

JOINING PARTS

Sew the head to the body.
Put the collar around the neck and tie it

Sew the sleeves to rnd 39 on both sides.

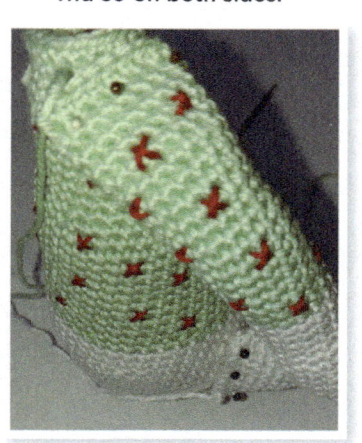

Sew the legs on both sides between rnd 9-12.

FINAL PHOTOS

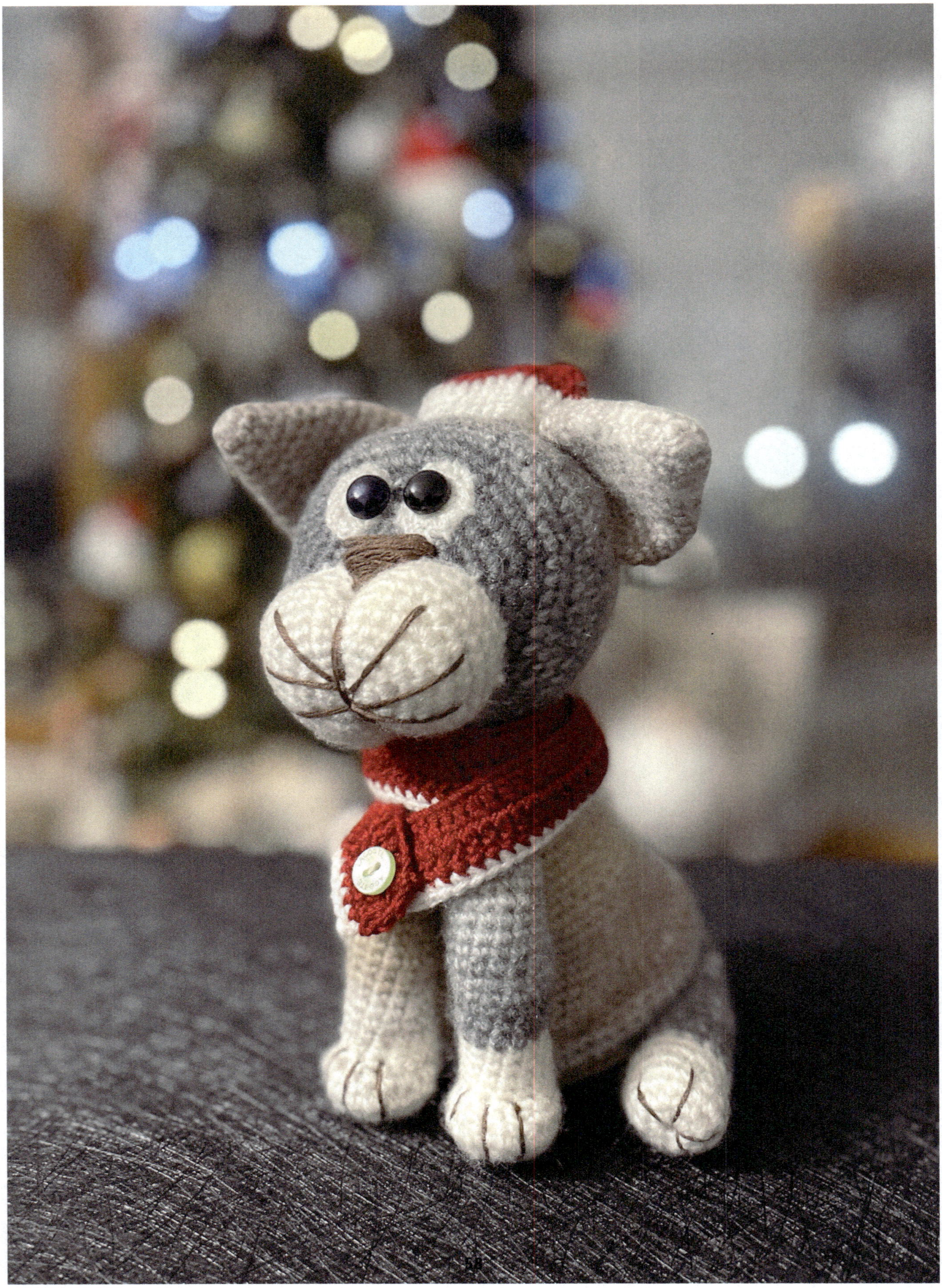

Abbreviation/US terminology :

blo	-	back loop
ch	-	chain
cr	-	crochet
dc	-	double crochet
dc3tog	-	double crochet three together
dec	-	decrease
flo	-	front loop
hdc	-	half double crochet
FO	-	Fasten Off
inc	-	increase
rnd(s)	-	round(s)
sc	-	single crochet
sc3tog	-	single crochet three together
slst	-	slip stitch
st	-	stitch
tr	-	treble stitch
(...)	-	number in parentheses indicates the number of stitches at the end of the round
[...]	-	repeat instructions x times or to the end of the round
(...)	-	work the stitches all into the same stitch

You are welcome to sell items made from this pattern. I would be happy if you link back to my shop and give credit to me as the designer.

Materials:

- Yarn
- 2.5 mm hook size or a size that fits your yarn
- Scissors, stuffing, tapestry needle, stitch marker and pins

Main Color: Brown White Grey Mixed Yarn **A:** Red **B:** White

FINISHED SIZE
Around 20 cm in circumference, about 10 cm in length.

HEAD

MAIN COLOR

Rnd 1-6 sc in mr

Rnd 2-6 sc inc(12)

Rnd 3-(6 times)1 sc into sc next inc(18)

Rnd 4-(6 times)2 sc into sc next inc(24)

Rnd 5-(6 times)3 sc into sc next inc(30)

Rnd 6-(6 times)4 sc into sc next inc(36)

Rnd 7-(6 times)5 sc into sc next inc(42)

Rnd 8-(6 times)6 sc into sc next inc(48)

Rnd 9-(6 times)7 sc into sc next inc(54)

Rnd 10-20-(11 ring)sc into sc(54)

Rnd 21-(6 times)7 sc into sc next dec(48)

Rnd 22-(6 times)6 sc into sc next dec(42)

Rnd 23-(6 times)5 sc into sc next dec(36)

Rnd 24-(6 times)4 sc into sc next dec(30)

Rnd 25-(6 times)3 sc into sc next dec(24)

Rnd 26-(6 times)2 sc into sc next dec(18)

Rnd 27-(6 times)1 sc into sc next dec(12)

Rnd 28-6 sc dec fo.Clean the thread end.

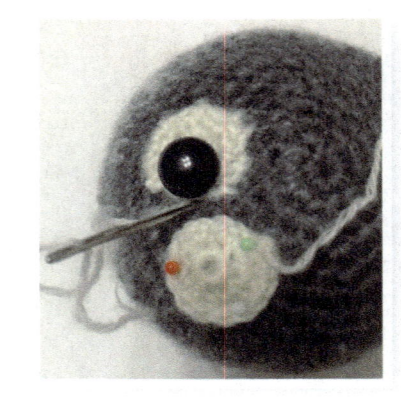

NOSE

B COLOR

Rnd 1-6 sc in mr

Rnd 2-6 sc inc(12)

Rnd 3-(6 times)1 sc into sc next inc(18)

Rnd 4-(6 times)2 sc into sc next inc(24)

Rnd 5-(6 times)3 sc into sc next inc(30)

Rnd 6-(6 times)4 sc into sc next inc(36)

Rnd 7-(6 times)5 sc into sc next inc(42)

Rnd 8-11-(4 ring)sc into sc(42)fo.Leave a long thread end to sew.

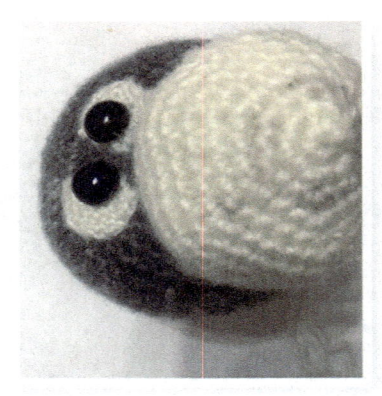

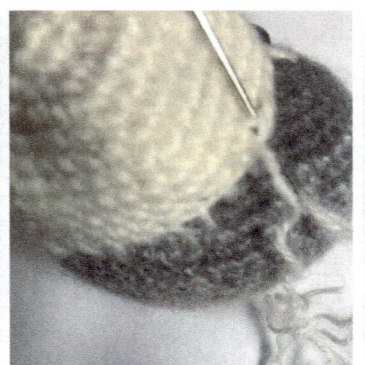

BODY

MAIN COLOR

Rnd 1-6 sc in mr

Rnd 2-6 sc inc(12)

Rnd 3-(6 times)1 sc into sc next inc(18)

Rnd 4-(6 times)2 sc into sc next inc(24)

Rnd 5-(6 times)3 sc into sc next inc(30)

Rnd 6-(6 times)4 sc into sc next inc(36)

Rnd 7-(6 times)5 sc into sc next inc(42)

Rnd 8-(6 times)6 sc into sc next inc(48)

Rnd 9-(6 times)7 sc into sc next inc(54)

Rnd 10-sc into sc(54)

Rnd 11-İn flo sc into sc(54)

Rnd 12-17-(6 ring)sc into sc(54)

Rnd 18-(6 times)7 sc into sc next dec(48)

Rnd 19-24-(6 ring)sc into sc(48)

Rnd 25-(6 times)6 sc into sc next dec(42)

Rnd 26-31-(6 ring)sc into sc(42)

Rnd 32-(6 times)5 sc into sc next dec(36)

Rnd 33-sc into sc(36)

Rnd 34-11 sc into sc Bring legs together and first leg 7 sc second leg 7 sc (14)11 sc into sc(36) Fill the hull and keep filling as you go.

Rnd 35-(6 times)4 sc into sc next dec(30)

Rnd 36-sc into sc(30)

Rnd 37-(6 times)3 sc into sc next dec(24)

Rnd 38-(6 times)2 sc into sc next dec(18)

Rnd 39-40-(2 ring)sc into sc(18)fo.Leave a long thread end to sew.

HIND LEGS

MAIN COLOR - MAKE 2

Rnd 1-7 sc in mr

Rnd 2-7 sc inc(14)

Rnd 3-16-(12 ring)sc into sc(14)

Rnd 17-Flatten and sink the awl into both layers. 6 sc fo.

Leave a long thread end to sew.

EARS

MAIN COLOR - MAKE 2

Rnd 1-6 sc in mr

Rnd 2-2 sc into sc next inc(8)

Rnd 3-3 sc into sc next inc(10)

Rnd 4-2 sc inc(12)

Rnd 5-2 sc inc(14)

Rnd 6-2 sc inc(16)

Rnd 7-2 sc inc(18)

Rnd 8-2 sc inc(20)

Rnd 9-2 sc inc(22)

Rnd 10-2 sc inc(24)

Rnd 11-sc into sc(24)

Rnd 12-Flatten and sink the awl into both layers.

11 sc fo.Leave a long thread end to sew.

TAIL

MAIN COLOR

Rnd 1-7 sc in mr

Rnd 2-7 sc inc(14)

Rnd 3-7-(5 ring)sc into sc(14) Fill the queue.

Keep filling as you go.

Rnd 8-(2 times)6 sc into sc next dec(12)

Rnd 9-32-(24 ring)sc into sc(12)

Rnd 33-Flatten and sink the awl into both layers.

5 sc fo.Leave a long thread end to sew.

JOINING PARTS

Sew the ears on both sides between Rnd 17 and 18. There should be 10 sc between them.

Sew the white part of the eye to Rnd 3. Sew the buttons onto the white part of the eye.

Sew the nose under the eyes and fill in the inside.

Sew the hind legs between Rnd 5-10 on both sides.

HAT

B COLOR

Rnd 1-6 sc in mr

Rnd 2-6 sc inc(12)

Rnd 3-6-(4 ring)sc into sc(12)

Rnd 7-6 sc dec(6)

Rnd 8-sc into sc(6) A COLOR

Rnd 9-6 sc inc(12)

Rnd 10-21-(12 ring)sc into sc(12)

Rnd 22-2 sc inc(14)

Rnd 23-2 sc inc(16)

Rnd 24-2 sc inc(18)

Rnd 25-2 sc inc(20)

Rnd 26-2 sc inc(22)

Rnd 27-2 sc inc(24)

Rnd 28-2 sc inc(26)

Rnd 29-2 sc inc(28)

Rnd 30-2 sc inc(30) B COLOR

Rnd 31-(6 times)3 sc into sc next inc(36)

Rnd 32-sc into cr(36)fo.Leave a long thread end to sew.

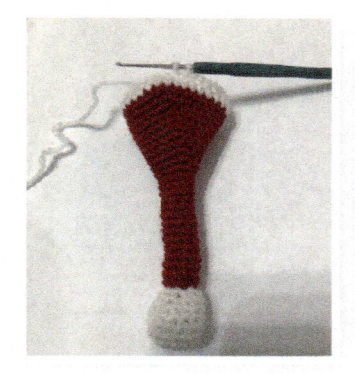

SCARF

A COLOR

Rnd 1-86 ch turn

Rnd 2-85 ch into cr 2 ch turn

Rnd 3-cr into cr 2 ch turn B color-

Rnd 4-cr into sc(85 sc)fo.

FINAL PHOTOS

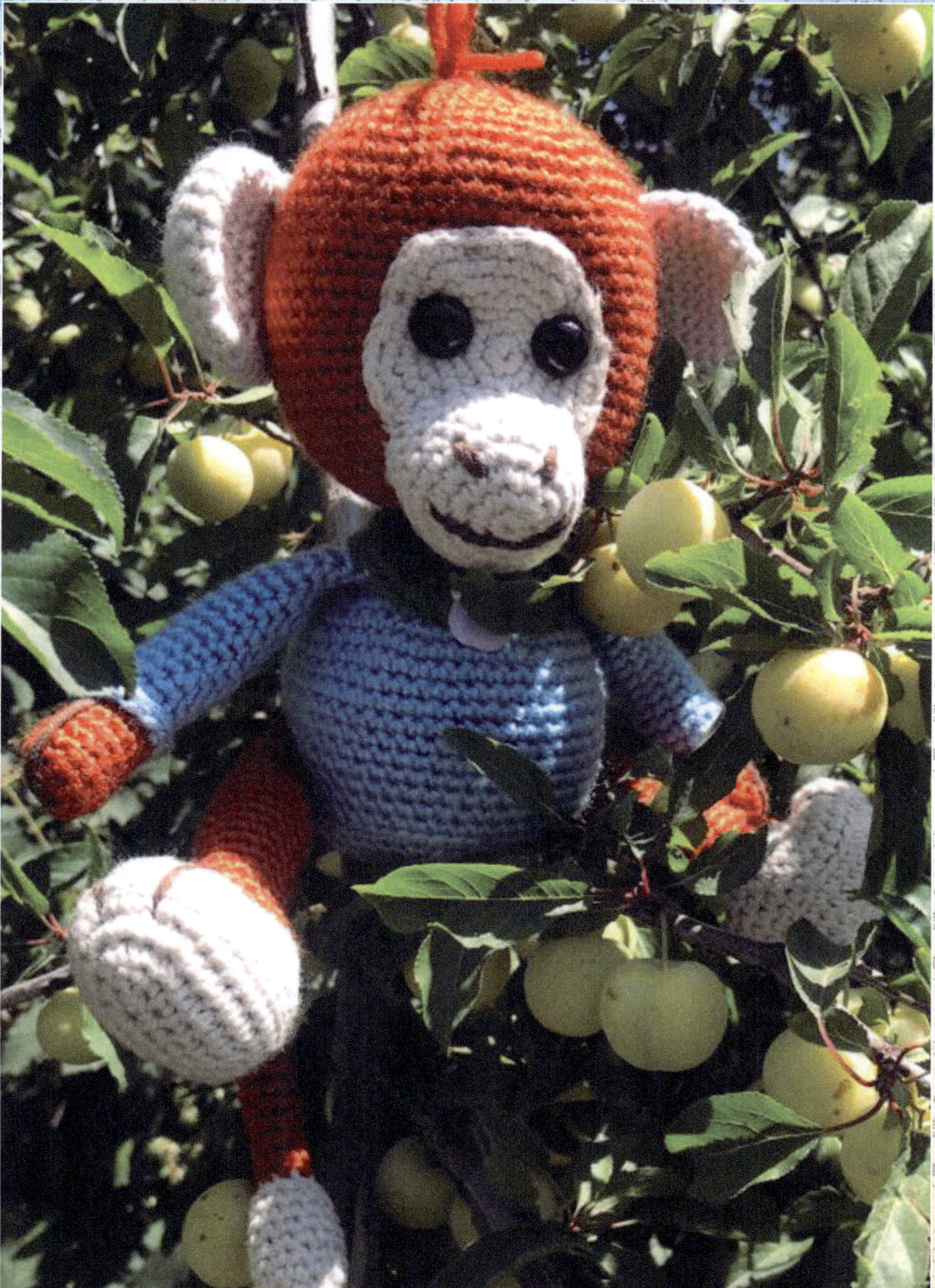

Abbreviation/US terminology :

blo	-	back loop
ch	-	chain
cr	-	crochet
dc	-	double crochet
dc3tog	-	double crochet three together
dec	-	decrease
flo	-	front loop
hdc	-	half double crochet
FO	-	Fasten Off
inc	-	increase
rnd(s)	-	round(s)
sc	-	single crochet
sc3tog	-	single crochet three together
slst	-	slip stitch
st	-	stitch
tr	-	treble stitch
(...)	-	number in parentheses indicates the number of stitches at the end of the round
[...]	-	repeat instructions x times or to the end of the round
(...)	-	work the stitches all into the same stitch

You are welcome to sell items made from this pattern. I would be happy if you link back to my shop and give credit to me as the designer.

Materials:

- Yarn
- 2.5 mm hook size or a size that fits your yarn
- Scissors, stuffing, tapestry needle, stitch marker and pins

Main Color: Orange **A:** Cream Color **B:** Light Blue

FINISHED SIZE
Around 20 cm in circumference, about 10 cm in length.

HEAD AND BODY

MAIN COLOR

R 1-6 sc in a mr

R 2-6 sc inc(12)

R 3-(6 times) 1 sc into sc next inc(18)

R 4-(6 times) 2 sc into sc next inc(24)

R 5-(6 times)3 sc into sc next inc(30)

R 6-(6 times)4 sc into sc next inc(36)

R 7-(6 times)5 sc into sc next inc(42)

R 8-(6 times)6 sc into sc next inc(48)

R 9-23-(15 ring)sc into sc(48)

R 24-(6 times)6 sc into sc next dec(42)

R 25-(6 times)5 sc into sc next dec(36)

R 26-(6 times)4 sc into sc next dec(30)

R 27-(6 times)3 sc into sc next dec(24)

R 28-(6 times)2 sc into sc next dec(18)

R 29-32-(4 ring)sc into sc(18)

BODY - B COLOR

R 33-(6 times)2 sc into sc next inc(24)

R 34-(6 times)3 sc into sc next inc(30)

R 35-(6 times)4 sc into sc next inc(36)

R 36-(6 times)5 sc into sc next inc(42)

R 37-48-(12 ring)sc into sc(42)

R 49-İn blo sc into sc(42)

R 50-(6 times)5 sc into sc next dec(36)

R 51-(6 times)4 sc into sc next dec(30)

R 52-(6 times)3 sc into sc next dec(24)

Tightly fill the body

R 53-(6 times)2 sc into sc next dec(18)

R 54-(6 times)1 sc into sc next dec(12)

R 55-6 sc dec fo.Clean the thread end.

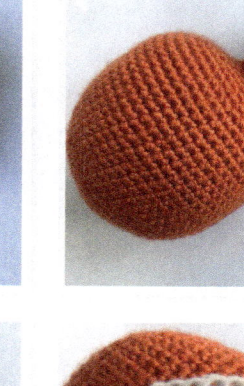

EARS

MAKE 2 - A COLOR

R 1-6 sc in a mr

R 2-6 sc inc(12)

R 3-(6 times)1 sc into sc next inc(18)

R 4-(6 times)2 sc into sc next inc(24)

R 5-8-(4 ring)sc into sc (24)

R 9-(6 times)2 sc into sc next dec(18)

R 10-Combine. sink the needle into both layers

sc fo.

Leave a long thread end to sew.

FACE

A COLOR

R 1-6 sc in a mr

R 2-6 sc inc(12)

R 3-(6 times)1 sc into sc next inc(18)

R 4-(6 times)2 sc into sc next inc(24)

R 5-(6 times)3 sc into sc next inc(30)

R 6-(6 times)4 sc into sc next inc(36)fo.

Leave a long thread end to sew.

NOSE

A COLOR

R 1-6 sc in a mr

R 2-6 sc inc(12)

R 3-(6 times)1 sc into sc next inc(18)

R 4-(6 times)2 sc into sc next inc(24)

R 5-8-(4 ring)sc into sc(24)fo

Leave a long thread end to sew.

Fill the nose.

ARMS

MAIN COLOR

R 1-6 sc in a mr

R 2-6 sc inc(12)

R 3-7-(5 ring)sc into sc(12)

R 8-B color-İn flo sc into sc(12)

R 9-23-(15 ring)sc into sc(12)

R 24-Straighten it. sink the needle into both layers

6 sc fo. Leave a long thread end to sew.

ARMS DETAILS -R 8-İn blo sc into sc(12)

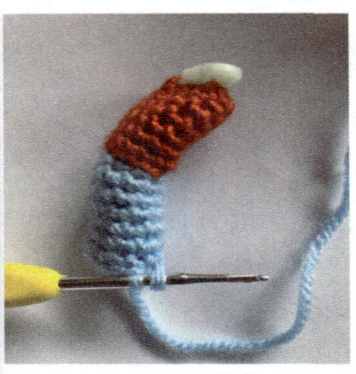

LEGS

A COLOR

R 1-9 ch.Turn

R 2-8 ch inc(16)

R 3-(8 times)1 sc into sc next inc(24)

R 3-(8 times)2 sc into sc next inc(32)

R 4-6(3 ring)sc into sc(32)

R 7-10 sc into sc(9 sc dec)10 sc into sc(22)

R 8-8 sc into sc(6 sc dec)8 sc into sc(16)

MAIN COLOR

R 9-27-(19 ring)sc into sc(16)

R 28-Straighten it. sink the needle into both layers

7 sc fo. Leave a long thread end to sew.

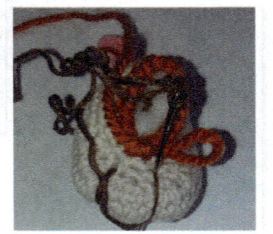

TAIL & COLLAR

A COLOR

R 1-6 sc in a mr

R 2-6 sc inc(12)

R 3-7-(5 ring)sc into sc(12)

R 8-4 sc dec(8)Fill the tail end

R 9-34(25 ring)sc into sc(8)Fo.Leave a long thread end to sew.

COLLAR - C COLOR

R 1-22 ch.

R 2-21 ch into cr fo.Leave a long thread end to sew.

JOINING PARTS

Sew the ears to both sides between R 10-18

sew the sleeves sideways to R 33

Sew the legs on both sides between R 44-48

sew tail back to R 49

Attach the eyes to the face of the R 18.

FINAL PHOTOS

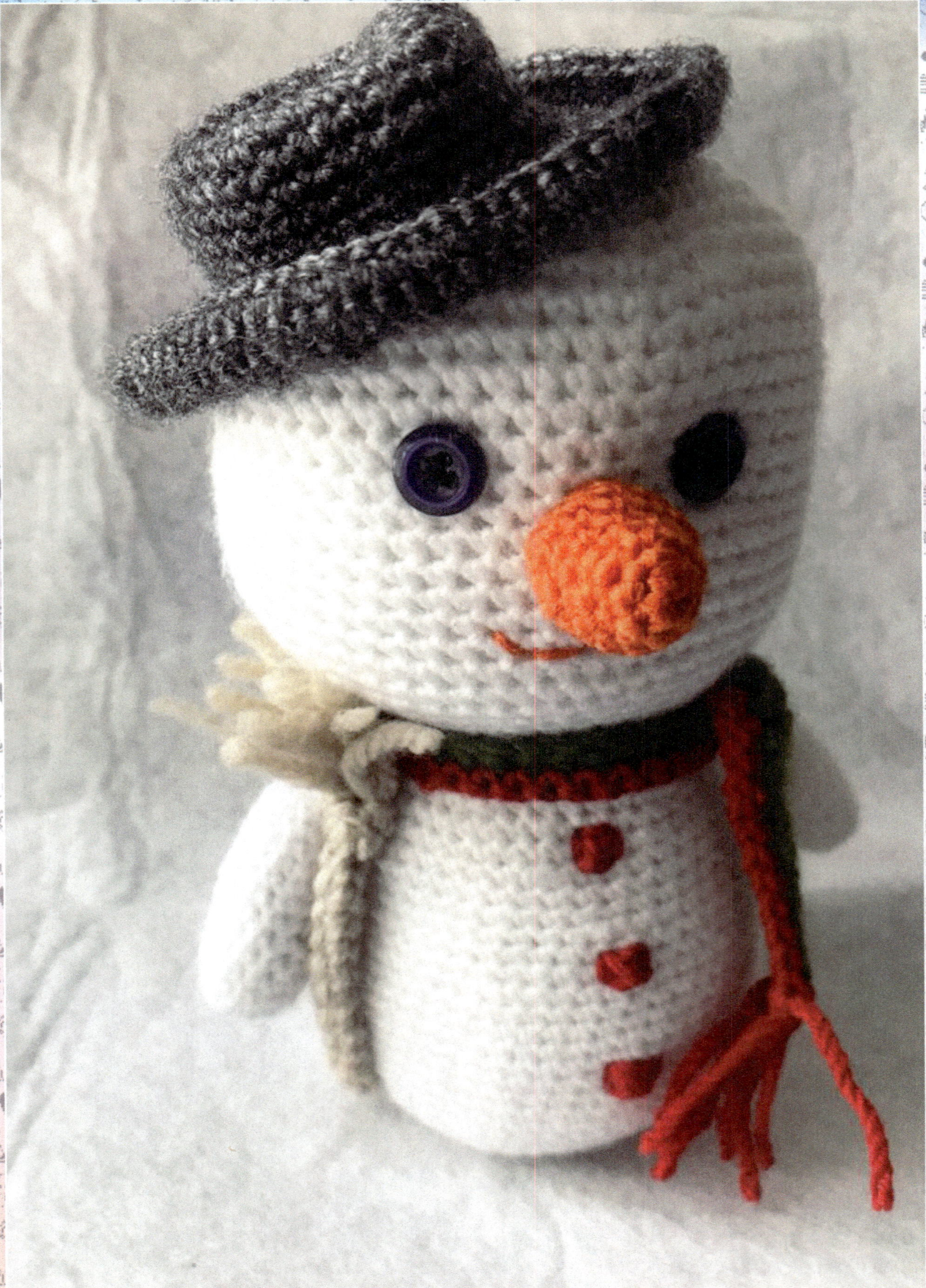

Abbreviation/US terminology :

blo	-	back loop
ch	-	chain
cr	-	crochet
dc	-	double crochet
dc3tog	-	double crochet three together
dec	-	decrease
flo	-	front loop
hdc	-	half double crochet
FO	-	Fasten Off
inc	-	increase
rnd(s)	-	round(s)
sc	-	single crochet
sc3tog	-	single crochet three together
slst	-	slip stitch
st	-	stitch
tr	-	treble stitch
(...)	-	number in parentheses indicates the number of stitches at the end of the round
[...]	-	repeat instructions x times or to the end of the round
(...)	-	work the stitches all into the same stitch

Materials:

- Yarn
- 2.5 mm hook size or a size that fits your yarn
- Scissors, stuffing, tapestry needle, stitch marker and pins

Main Color: White **A:** Smoked Color **B:** Green **C:** Red **D:** Orange
E: Light Brown

FINISHED SIZE
Around 20 cm in circumference, about 10 cm in length.

You are welcome to sell items made from this pattern.
I would be happy if you link back to my shop and give
credit to me as the designer.

HEAD & BODY

MAIN COLOR

Rnd 1-6 sc in mr

Rnd 2-6 sc inc(12)

Rnd 3-(6 times)1 sc into sc next inc(18)

Rnd 4-(6 times)2 sc inc(24)

Rnd 5-(6 times)3 sc inc(30)

Rnd 6-(6 times)4 sc inc(36)

Rnd 7-(6 times)5 sc inc(42)

Rnd 8-(6 times)6 sc inc(48)

Rnd 9-(6 times)7 sc inc(54)

Rnd 10-26-(17 ring)sc into sc(54)

Rnd 27-(6 times)7 sc into sc next dec(48)

Rnd 28-(6 times)6 sc dec(42)

Rnd 29-(6 times)5 sc dec(36)

Rnd 30-(6 times)4 sc dec(30)

Rnd 31-sc into sc(30) fill the head

Rnd 32-(6 times)4 sc inc(36)

Rnd 33-(6 times)5 sc inc(42)

Rnd 34-(6 times)6 sc inc(48)

Rnd 35-39-(5 ring)sc into sc(48)

Rnd 40-(6 times)7 sc inc(54)

Rnd 41-42-(2 ring)sc into sc(54)

Rnd 43-(6 times)8 sc inc(60)

Rnd 44-55-(12 ring)sc into sc(60)

Rnd 56-(6 times)8 sc into sc next dec(54)

Rnd 57-(6 times)7 sc dec(48)

Rnd 59-(6 times)6 sc dec(42)

Rnd 60-(6 times)5 sc dec(36)Fill the body

Rnd 61-(6 times)4 sc dec(30)

Rnd 62-(6 times)3 sc dec(24)

Rnd-63-(6 times)2 sc dec(18)

Rnd 64-(6 times)1 sc dec(12)

Rnd 65-6 sc dec fo.clean the thread end

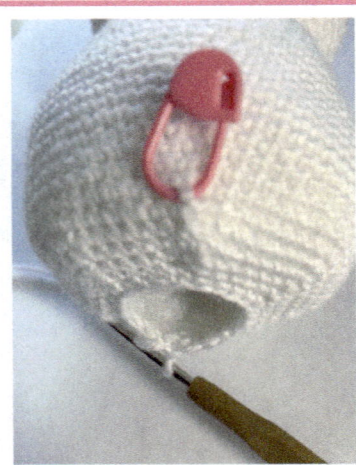

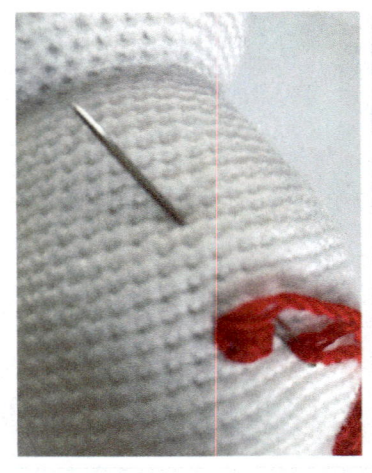

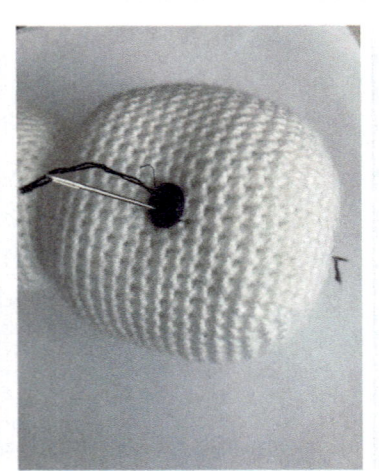

HAT

A COLOR

R 1-6 sc in a mr

R 2-6 sc inc(12)

R 3-(6 times)1 sc into sc next inc(18)

R 4-(6 times)2 sc inc(24)

R 5-(6 times)3 sc inc(30)

R 6-(6 times)4 sc inc(36)

R 7-(6 times)5 sc inc(42)

R 8-14-(7 ring)sc into sc(42)

R 15-42 sc inc(84)

R 16-20-(5 ring)sc into sc(84)fo.

NOSE

D COLOR

R 1-6 sc in mr

R 2-sc into sc(6)

R 3-2 sc inc(8)

R 4-sc into sc(8)

R 5-2 sc inc(10)

R 6-sc into sc(10)

R 7-2 sc inc(12)

R 8-9-(2 ring)sc into sc(12)fo.

Leave a long thread end to sew.

SCARF

B COLOR

R 1-71 ch turn

R 2-70 ch into sc(70)1 ch turn

C color-

R 3-sc into sc fo.

Kollar-Ana color 2 tane yapın

R 1-6 sc in mr

R 2-6 sc inc(12)

R 3-15-(13 ring)sc into sc(12)

R 16-Straighten it. Dip the awl into both layers.5 sc fo.

Leave a long thread end to sew.

MOP

E COLOR

R 1-16 ch turn

R 2-15 ch into sc 1 ch turn

R 3-sc into sc fo.Leave a long thread end to sew.

JOINING PARTS

Sew the eyes between Rnd 14-15

Sew between Nose Rnd 16-19 fill the nose

Sew sleeves to Rnd 32.

FINAL PHOTOS

Dear Customer
I am on emerging editor and, with the sales made by the book,
I can continue my studies to publish
other books on the subject.
I would appreciate on honest review from you. Also, please if
you notice any mistakes or missing
information, feel free to contact me at this
e-mail address: wwwanacraft@gmail.com
Thank you for your support

write to us to get extra free content for you

https://forms.gle/BoTwQKSR3nwhHc2X9

Printed in Great Britain
by Amazon